New International Business English

Communication skills in English for business purposes

Student's Book

Leo Jones

Richard Alexander

CAMBRIDGE
UNIVERSITY PRESS

Published by the Press Syndicate of the University of Cambridge
The Pitt Building, Trumpington Street, Cambridge CB2 1RP
40 West 20th Street, New York, NY 10011–4211, USA
10 Stamford Road, Oakleigh, Melbourne 3166, Australia

© Cambridge University Press 1989, 1996

First published 1989
New Edition 1996
Seventh printing 1998

Some of the names of companies and individuals in this book are
fictitious. In these cases any resemblance to an actual company or
person is coincidental.

Printed in Great Britain
at the University Press, Cambridge

A catalogue record for this book is available from the British Library

ISBN 0 521 45580 4 Student's Book
ISBN 0 521 45577 4 Student's Book Cassette Set
ISBN 0 521 45579 0 Workbook
ISBN 0 521 45578 2 Workbook Cassette Set
ISBN 0 521 45576 6 Teacher's Book
ISBN 0 521 42735 5 Video Teacher's Guide
ISBN 0 521 42732 0 Video Cassette (VHS PAL)
ISBN 0 521 42733 9 Video Cassette (VHS SECAM)
ISBN 0 521 42734 7 Video Cassette (VHS NTSC)

Contents

Thanks

We'd like to say a big 'Thank You' to everyone who helped us, made comments and suggestions, and who encouraged us while we were working on this project:

Will Capel, our editor, started the ball rolling and kept the project moving along. His critical comments encouraged us to incorporate innumerable improvements.

Alison Silver guided the project smoothly, efficiently and cheerfully towards its publication. Her eye for detail, good humour, encouragement and thoroughness enhanced the book enormously. Working with her was, as always, a delight.

Amanda Ogden devoted great care and attention to researching the photographs and obtaining permission for us to use the reading texts.

Ruth Carim for her eagle-eyed proof-reading.

Nick Newton and Randell Harris designed the book with good taste and flair.

Martin Williamson produced the recordings and the engineer was Jerry Peal at Studio AVP.

The actors who participated in the recording sessions.

All the teachers who gave us feedback on the First Edition – and contributed their own suggestions and ideas for improvements. In particular, thanks to:

Stephen Berg and Paulo Gilberto de Araujo Galarti in Brazil;
Alison Haill and Sue Pedley in England;
J. Dantreveaux, Patrick Foley, Robin Forrest, Susan Hendrie, Jeffrey Hill,
Matt Norton, Carolyne Occhuzzo, David Podger, Jeanette Ramos, Anita Subtil,
J. Vernon and M. Weber in France;
Irene Bruntsch, A. Dördelmann-Stappert, Christine Frank, Sarah Jones-Macziola,
Eberhard Kelin, John Riach, Inge Spaughton and Douglas L. Sperry in Germany;
Aouda Au, Jonathan Hull, Regina Lo and Raymond Ng in Hong Kong;
Péter Koronváry and Monika Szabó in Hungary;
Anne Brindle and Christine Calvert in Italy;
Leonard Crawford and Tessa Pacey in Japan;
Peter Ellis, Nick Flynn, Joanne Foxford, Thérèse Kennedy, Richard Lane and
Cees Sier in Spain;
Pam Scott in Thailand;
Colin Sowden in Wales.

Finally, thanks from Leo to Sue, Zoë and Thomas, and from Richard to Gerlinde, for their support behind the scenes.

Introduction

Who is this book for?

◆ *New International Business English* is for business people who need to, or will soon need to, use English in their work. It is also designed to be used by adult students who will be entering the world of business at the end of their course of studies.

What is 'Business English'?

◆ Although there is a certain amount of vocabulary that you could call 'business vocabulary', most business English is simply *English used in business contexts* – it is not a special language. Every industry (and to some extent, each company or even department) uses a special 'jargon' and such specialized terminology can't be covered in a book of this kind.

   What we do provide is a wide range of business settings and situations in which you can practise and improve your communication skills in English, so that you can become more confident, more fluent and more accurate.

What's in the Student's Book?

◆ Units 1 to 4 introduce the BASIC BUSINESS ENGLISH SKILLS that are essential whatever you're doing in business. These skills will be further practised and expanded in later units. Students who already have practical experience of using English in business may be able to go more rapidly through these early units than students with less experience.
◆ Units 5 to 14 are based on INTEGRATED ACTIVITIES. They assume a familiarity with the basic skills introduced and practised in the first four units. Each unit covers different business situations, and practises a wide range of business skills.
◆ Unit 15 revises many of the skills introduced and practised in previous units. It takes the form of a SIMULATION.
◆ FILES: if you look at the back of the book (pages 146 to 175), you'll see that there are 85 'Files', which appear to be arranged in random order. In some activities in the book you'll be directed to a particular File at the back of the book. Here you'll be given information to act upon or information about the role you'll have to play. Your partner will be directed to a different File, so that you each see different information and there is a realistic 'information gap' between you. You'll have to react spontaneously to what your partner tells you – just as in real life.

What do the units contain?

◆ INTEGRATED ACTIVITIES: these include reading, listening and writing tasks, as well as discussion, problem-solving and role-play.
◆ ROLE-PLAY (shown like this: 🖾) is an essential part of the course. Many tasks also involve simulated telephone conversations (shown like this: 🖾). Most parts of the integrated activities are done in pairs or small groups, so that everyone has a chance to participate.
◆ VOCABULARY is introduced in context through the texts and exercises.
◆ FUNCTIONS sections introduce and practise the functional language required in business situations.

◆ READING tasks are integrated within the activities, but in some units there is a separate section, always leading to a discussion.
◆ ◎◎ LISTENING tasks are integrated within the activities – this sometimes involves hearing a phone call, and then taking and relaying a message.
◆ DISCUSSION: in every unit discussion follows naturally from an activity or exercise – there are plenty of opportunities for discussion throughout the book.

What's in the Workbook and on the Workbook recordings?

◆ BACKGROUND KNOWLEDGE sections, giving information for students who have little or no experience of using English in their work. These explain the background to the business situations practised in each unit.
◆ GRAMMAR sections revising the main 'problem areas' of English grammar, with exercises based on business situations.
◆ Follow-up FUNCTIONS exercises, some of which are recorded on the Workbook recordings.
◆ Follow-up exercises on VOCABULARY.
◆ Supplementary exercises:
  – PREPOSITIONS and phrasal verbs
  – WRITING tasks on letters, faxes, reports, etc.
  – LISTENING tasks, based on the Workbook recordings
  – READING comprehension exercises
◆ An ANSWER KEY with model answers to all the exercises.

As you work through the Student's Book and Workbook, always try to relate your own personal knowledge and experience to the activities and exercises you're doing – this may be background knowledge you've studied, or practical knowledge from your own work experience or professional life.

We hope you enjoy using *New International Business English*!

Leo Jones   Richard Alsalu

1 Face to face

1.1 First impressions ...

A *Work in pairs* Imagine that these people are greeting you when you arrive as a visitor in an unfamiliar office. Discuss these questions with your partner:

- What impression does each person give?
- Which person seems the most welcoming?

B ◎◎ You'll hear each person above talking to a visitor.

Work in pairs Discuss these questions with your partner:

- Which of the visitors are greeted in a friendly and efficient way?
- Which of the visitors are made to feel welcome?
- What made the unwelcoming people seem unfriendly or unhelpful?

C *Work in groups* Discuss these questions with your partners:

- What impression do you try to give to the people you deal with in business?
- What impression do you try *not* to give?
- Add some more adjectives to these lists:

I try to be: *pleasant sincere efficient* ....
I try NOT to be: *unfriendly shy aggressive* ....

➡ What *exactly* would you say when you greet a visitor to your office?

D 🔊 You'll hear three conversations in which people are meeting and being introduced to each other.

Listen to what they say to each other and fill the gaps below:

1   *Alex White, a new employee, meets Chris Grey.*

   Alex White: I'd just like to   introduce myself   . My name's Alex White and I'm the new export sales co-ordinator.

   Chris Grey: Oh, yes. I've heard of you. How   ? I'm Chris Grey.   you. …

2   *Liz Jones, a colleague from Canada, is visiting the office in London.*

   Tony Harris: Ms Smith, I'd   Mrs Jones. Mrs Jones is from our sales office in Toronto.

   Liz Jones: Hi!

   Claire Smith: , Mrs Jones? I've been   meeting you.

   Liz Jones: Oh, please   Liz.

   Claire Smith: And I'm Claire.

   Liz Jones: Hi.

   Claire Smith: Well, Liz, did you   ?

   Liz Jones: Yeah, not too bad. …

3   *Miss Lucas, a visitor from Argentina, is introduced to Mr Evans.*

   Mrs Green: Mr Evans,   Miss Lucas? She's from Argentina.

   Mr Evans: Yes, I think we've met before. It's   !

   Miss Lucas: That's right, hello again.   ?

   Mr Evans: Fine, thanks. …

➡ *Work in pairs* Listen to the conversations again and notice how the 'small talk' (social conversation) develops. Discuss how each conversation might continue.

> Here are some questions that you could ask a new colleague or client if you want to be friendly and start a conversation:
>
> | | |
> |---|---|
> | *Did you have a good journey?* | *Is this your first visit to …?* |
> | *Do you need any help or information?* | *When did you actually arrive?* |
> | *Where are you staying?* | *Whereabouts do you come from in …?* |

E 🗣 The class is divided into two teams. If you're in the A Team, look at File **1** on page 146. If you're in the B Team, look at File **31** on page 156. Follow the instructions in your File.

F *Work in small groups* Ask your partners:

What do you find difficult or enjoyable about talking to …

… someone you've never met before?
… a superior or head of department?
… someone who is considerably older than you?
… people from different countries?   (Consider several different nationalities.)
… a large group of people?

A *Work in pairs* What do you call someone who comes from each of these countries?

Australia	Canada	Holland	India	Norway	Sweden
Brazil	France	Hungary	New Zealand	Saudi Arabia	the USA

> If he comes from Scotland he's a Scotsman.
> If they come from Italy they're Italians.
> If she comes from Ireland she's an Irishwoman.
> If he comes from Pakistan he's a Pakistani.

B *Work in pairs* Make a list of the following countries. Be careful about your spelling!

5 African countries
......Nigeria........ ....

5 Asian countries
....

5 countries in the Middle East
....

5 Latin American countries
....

5 countries belonging to the European Union (EU)
....

5 European countries which don't belong to the EU
....

➡ When you're ready, join another pair. Ask them to tell you what they would call a person from each of the countries on your list.

C **1** *Work in groups or as a class* Discuss these questions:
- If someone comes from another country, what differences do you expect in their behaviour, manners, eating habits, etc.? Think of some examples.
- Which other nationalities do you think are *most* different from your own? Give your reasons.

2 Read this article and choose one of these titles for it:

When in Rome ...	**Problems that business people face**
Travelling abroad	**Good manners, good business**
Doing business in Europe	**I didn't mean to be rude!**

NOBODY actually wants to cause offence but, as business becomes ever more international, it is increasingly easy to get it wrong. There may be a single European market but it does not mean that managers behave the same in Greece as they do in Denmark.

In many European countries handshaking is an automatic gesture. In France good manners require that on arriving at a business meeting a manager shakes hands with everyone present. This can be a demanding task and, in a crowded room, may require gymnastic ability if the farthest hand is to be reached.

Handshaking is almost as popular in other countries – including Germany, Belgium and Italy. But Northern Europeans, such as the British and Scandinavians, are not quite so fond of physical demonstrations of friendliness.

In Europe the most common challenge is not the content of the food, but the way you behave as you eat. Some things are just not done. In France it is not good manners to raise tricky questions of business over the main course. Business has its place: after the cheese course. Unless you are prepared to eat in silence you have to talk about something – something, that is, other than the business deal which you are continually chewing over in your head.

Italians give similar importance to the whole process of business entertaining. In fact, in Italy the biggest fear, as course after course appears, is that you entirely forget you are there on business. If you have the energy, you can always do the polite thing when the meal finally ends, and offer to pay. Then, after a lively discussion, you must remember the next polite thing to do – let your host pick up the bill.

In Germany, as you walk sadly back to your hotel room, you may wonder why your apparently friendly hosts have not invited you out for the evening. Don't worry, it is probably nothing personal. Germans do not entertain business people with quite the same enthusiasm as some of their European counterparts.

The Germans are also notable for the amount of formality they bring to business. As an outsider, it is often difficult to know whether colleagues have been working together for 30 years or have just met in the lift. If you are used to calling people by their first names this can be a little strange. To the Germans, titles are important. Forgetting that someone should be called *Herr Doktor* or *Frau Direktorin* might cause serious offence. It is equally offensive to call them by a title they do not possess.

In Italy the question of title is further confused by the fact that everyone with a university degree can be called *Dottore* – and engineers, lawyers and architects may also expect to be called by their professional titles.

These cultural challenges exist side by side with the problems of doing business in a foreign language. Language, of course, is full of difficulties – disaster may be only a syllable away. But the more you know of the culture of the country you are dealing with, the less likely you are to get into difficulties. It is worth the effort. It might be rather hard to explain that the reason you lost the contract was not the product or the price, but the fact that you offended your hosts in a light-hearted comment over an aperitif. Good manners are admired: they can also make or break the deal.

(Adapted from an article by Richard Bryan in *Business Life*)

3 Decide if these statements are true ☑ or false ☒, according to the writer:

1 In France you are expected to shake hands with everyone you meet. ☐
2 People in Britain shake hands just as much as people in Germany. ☐
3 In France people prefer talking about business during meals. ☐
4 It is not polite to insist on paying for a meal if you are in Italy. ☐
5 Visitors to Germany never get taken out for meals. ☐
6 German business people don't like to be called by their surnames. ☐
7 Make sure you know what the titles of the German people you meet are. ☐
8 Italian professionals are usually addressed by their titles. ☐
9 A humorous remark always goes down well all over the world. ☐

4 Discuss these questions:

- Which of the ideas in the article do you disagree with?
- What would you tell a foreign visitor about 'good manners' in your country?
- How much do you think international business is improved by knowing about foreign people's customs?

1.3 What do you enjoy about your work?

A ◎◎ You'll hear four people talking about their work. They work for Small World, a company that produces computer systems and software for handling maps and geographical information. Its customers include supermarket chains, local government departments and cable TV companies.

① As you listen for the first time, just note down below what the speakers' JOBS are – and what they don't enjoy about their work.

② Listen to the recording again. Note down your answers to the remaining questions.

③ Compare your notes with a partner.

Ian McShane is an

a

He is responsible for:

He enjoys:
1
2
3

He doesn't enjoy:

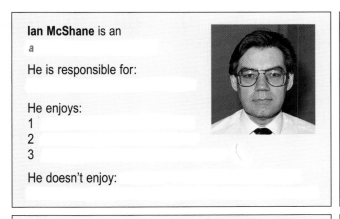

Lesley Trigg is an

a

Her responsibilities are:
1
2
3

She enjoys:

She doesn't enjoy:

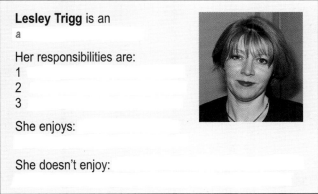

Patrick Verdon is a

s

administrator (this is a

t   -sh

kind of job).

His responsibilities include:
1
2   of machines, operating
   system and the software product.

He enjoys:

He doesn't enjoy: 1
                   2

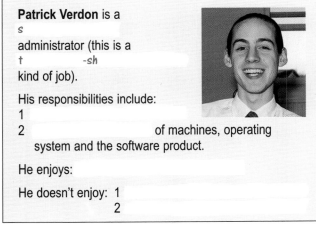

Paul Lockwood is a

t   o

He provides

for customers and agents.

He enjoys:
1
2
3

He doesn't enjoy:

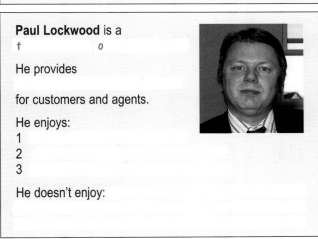

B **①** *Work in pairs* Ask your partner these questions:
- Which of the jobs that you have heard about would you most like to do yourself? Why?
- Which would you LEAST like to do? Why?

② Find out more about your partner's career. Ask about his or her:

> Work experience – previous jobs and any temporary or part-time jobs your partner has done
> Education and training
> Ambitions and prospects for the future
> Present job (if your partner is working) – its rewards and frustrations

➡ When you have both finished, tell the rest of the class what you have discovered.

1.4 It's not just what you say ...

A **1** *Work in pairs* Imagine that you're at a conference. Look at these name badges. If you're introduced to the man from London you'd say, *'Pleased to meet you, Mr Thomas'*, not *'Hello, Mr Howard'*. But what would you say to the other delegates?

Howard Thomas
LONDON

Lo Win Hao
TAIPEH

Rosa Burgos Garcia
VALENCIA

Kryskiewicz Grazyna
WARSAW

Ivany László
BUDAPEST

2 Try this quiz with your partner.

---

1 A good conversationalist is someone who ...
○ **a** always has plenty to say   ○ **b** has plenty of amusing stories to tell
○ **c** will listen carefully to what you have to say   ○ **d** asks a lot of questions

2 If someone looks you straight in the eye without blinking, they are probably ...
○ **a** honest   ○ **b** being rude   ○ **c** trying to frighten you   ○ **d** being friendly

3 If someone keeps looking out of the window while you're talking, they ...
○ **a** want to be outdoors   ○ **b** don't understand you   ○ **c** are not concentrating
○ **d** are thinking

4 If someone sighs while you're explaining something they are probably ...
○ **a** bored   ○ **b** impatient   ○ **c** unhappy   ○ **d** suffering from indigestion

5 If a man wearing jeans and a T-shirt comes into your office, he ...
○ **a** isn't correctly dressed   ○ **b** can't be important   ○ **c** is quite normal
○ **d** must be someone who has come to fix the phone or something

6 If someone shakes your hand very hard and long, they are ...
○ **a** pleased to see you   ○ **b** trying to show you that they are sincere
○ **c** waiting for you to say something   ○ **d** reliable and friendly

7 If a Canadian businessman keeps stepping backwards while he's talking to a Mexican businessman, this means that ...
○ **a** he doesn't like Mexicans   ○ **b** the Mexican is trying to be too friendly
○ **c** Northern people don't feel comfortable standing as close to another person as Southern people do
○ **d** Canadians are less friendly than Mexicans

8 If a Japanese person gives you their business card, you should hold it ...
○ **a** in your left hand   ○ **b** in your right hand   ○ **c** in both hands
○ **d** without reading it

"He won't be long. Can I get you endless cups of coffee?"

B *Work in groups* Discuss how the IMPRESSION you may give, especially to a stranger or to someone from another country, can be affected by:
- The noises you make: yawning   clicking a pen   sniffing   tapping your fingers
- Talking in a loud voice   talking in a soft voice
- Your body language and appearance, as shown in these pictures:

C *Work in groups* Ask your partners these questions:
- In your own workplace or place of study, who do you call by their first names, and who by their surnames?
- Are there people who use your first name but who *you* are expected to call by their surnames?
- Would this be any different with British, American or other foreign people you work with?
- Who do you talk to at work or college about your family and leisure activities? Which of your co-workers or fellow students do you meet socially?

1.5 Developing relationships

A ◎◎ *Work in pairs* You'll hear five short conversations between people who work in the same company. After hearing each conversation, discuss these questions with your partner:
- What is the relationship between the speakers?
- What are their jobs?
- What are they talking about?
- How does a relationship change as you get to know someone better?

B As you get to know someone, it's useful to find out what your common interests are. Then you can have a social conversation as well as 'talking shop' (talking about business).

Work in pairs Which of these topics do you talk about – and which do you not talk about – during a first meeting with a business associate?

sport ☐   politics ☐   your family ☐   business ☐
travel ☐   hobbies ☐   films ☐   the weather ☐
music ☐   your education ☐   religion ☐   TV ☐
other topics ....

And what difference does it make if the other person is:

a foreigner   a man   a woman   older than you
younger than you   senior to you   junior to you?

➡ Join another pair and compare your ideas.

C 🗣 ◎◎ *Work in pairs* You're going to role-play a meeting between two business associates. Imagine that one of you has travelled a long way to see the other. You only meet twice a year, but you've established a good relationship.

Before you start, decide what topics you're going to talk about in step ❸.

❶ One of you arrives in the other's office.

❷ Greet each other:

> *Hello again! How are you getting on?*
> *Lovely to see you again! How are things?*

> *I'm fine, thanks. How are you?*
> *Very well, thanks. And how about you?*

❸ Small talk until you decide it's time to get down to business …

> *Right, let's get down to business, shall we?*

> *Yes, all right.*

★★ DON'T ROLE-PLAY THE BUSINESS PHASE OF THE MEETING. ★★

❹ Imagine that time has passed before saying …

> *Right, I think that's agreed then.*

> *Yes, sure.*

❺ More small talk before you say goodbye and one of you leaves the office:

> *See you again soon, I hope!*
> *Goodbye and thanks for everything!*
> *Give my regards to …*

> *I'm glad we were able to meet.*
> *Have a good journey!*
> *Have a pleasant evening!*

➡ Role-play the next meeting between the same people six months later – this time the other person is the visitor. Follow the same five steps.

2 Letters, faxes and memos

2.1 Communicating in writing

A *Work in groups* Imagine the picture shows YOUR desk. Identify the different kinds of correspondence. Then discuss these questions:

- Which of the items would you attend to first? Put them in order of priority.
- What correspondence did you receive last week? What action did you have to take? Was any of the correspondence in English?
- What proportions of business correspondence do you RECEIVE and SEND by ...
  letter ....%   fax ....%   telex ....%   memo ....%   e-mail ....% ?

B **1** *Work in pairs* Read this memo. Decide who 'HGW' is and what his or her job is.

MEMORANDUM

From: HGW   To: Department managers
Date: 21/4/99   Subject: In-service English classes

1   From Monday 8 May English classes will be held in the Training Centre
    (room 3.17). There will be two groups: intermediate level (8.30–10.00) and
    advanced level (10.30–12.00). Please encourage your staff to attend one of
    the sessions. All teaching materials will be provided but students will be
    expected to do homework and preparation outside working hours.

2   Please send me the names of all interested staff by noon on Wednesday 26
    April. They will be given an informal oral test during the first week in May
    so that we can decide which of the classes is best for them.

3   The size of each class will be limited to 12 participants.

                                                        HGW

2 🔘🔘 Listen to a conversation on the same
subject as the memo. Note down the
differences between the two ways of
communicating the information.

C **1** *Work in pairs* What are
the relative advantages of
talking to someone
face-to-face and writing to
them? Add more points to
this chart:

Communicating with someone face-to-face

Advantages & pleasures	Disadvantages & difficulties
You can see their reactions	You have to think and react quickly

Communicating with someone in writing

Advantages & pleasures	Disadvantages & difficulties
You can take your time	

2 *Join another pair* Compare your notes. Then make a list of the relative merits of communicating in writing …

… internally by memo or by e-mail
… externally by letter or by fax or by telex

2.2 Names and addresses

A *Work in pairs* Look at these envelopes. Discuss these questions:
- How are the addresses laid out differently from the way an address is written in your country?
- How do you feel if you receive a letter with your name spelt wrong?
- What impression is given if the addressee's job title or address are incorrect on the envelope?

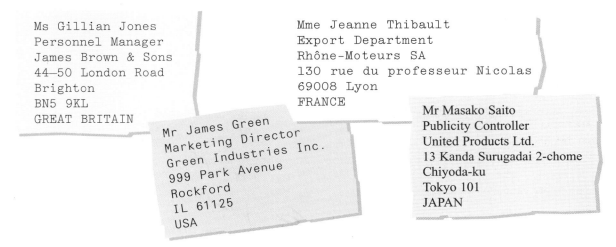

```
Ms Gillian Jones
Personnel Manager
James Brown & Sons
44—50 London Road
Brighton
BN5 9KL
GREAT BRITAIN
```

```
Mme Jeanne Thibault
Export Department
Rhône-Moteurs SA
130 rue du professeur Nicolas
69008 Lyon
FRANCE
```

```
Mr James Green
Marketing Director
Green Industries Inc.
999 Park Avenue
Rockford
IL 61125
USA
```

Mr Masako Saito
Publicity Controller
United Products Ltd.
13 Kanda Surugadai 2-chome
Chiyoda-ku
Tokyo 101
JAPAN

B ◎◎ You'll hear four addresses being dictated to you. Write down each address as if you're writing it on an envelope. (Later, you can check your answers in File **57**.)

C *Work in pairs* One of you should look at File **2**, the other at **33**. Dictate the addresses there to one another. You should S-P-E-L-L O-U-T any difficult words.

➡ Dictate YOUR OWN home and/or business address to your partner too.

"I have to be frank with you. Promotion prospects are terrible."

2.3 Layout and style

A *Work in pairs* This is the top part of a business letter. Decide when you would use these openings, instead of 'Dear Mr Green':

`Dear Jim,` `Dear Sir,` `Dear Madam,` `Dear Sir or Madam,`

UNIQUE PRODUCTS PLC
SUNRISE TECHNOLOGY PARK
WEST HARBOUR DRIVE
DOVER CT16 8KL
TELEPHONE 01306 824455   FAX 44 1306 821986

```
Mr James Green
Marketing Director
Green Industries Inc.
999 Park Avenue
Rockford
IL 61125
USA

Your Ref: GS/BC/44
Our Ref: DJ/GS/2                         11 November 1999

Dear Mr Green,

Thank you for your fax of 8 November, suggesting a meeting in
December. The most convenient dates from our point of view are
December 2nd or December 3rd.
```

➡ What are the differences between the layout above and the layout that is commonly used in your country (or in your company's 'house style')?

B Look at the endings of business letters below:
- When would you use the different styles and phrases?
- What do the abbreviations mean?
- Which of the styles and phrases would you find in American correspondence?
- If you begin your letter 'Dear Jim' how do you end it? If you begin 'Dear Sir' how do you end it?

```
Please let me know if this is
convenient.
Looking forward to hearing from you.

Best wishes,
Yours sincerely,
```
Gillian Jones
```
Ms Gillian Jones
Publicity Co-ordinator
```

Best regards,

Harry S. Bulstrode

Export Sales Manager

enc. Catalog and price list

```
Please phone us to confirm the details.
We look forward to receiving your comments.

Yours faithfully,
```
Maurice Tuttbright
```
p.p. Ms Gillian Jones
Publicity Co-ordinator
```

Sincerely,

H.S. Bulstrode

Export Sales Manager

c.c. Jane Sanchez

C **1** Highlight the ideas in this extract from a training manual that you think are most useful.

"GOLDEN RULES"

for writing letters (including faxes and memos)

1 Give your letter a heading (✦) if it will make it easier for the reader to understand your purpose in writing.

2 Decide what you are going to say before you start to write or dictate a letter, because if you don't do this the sentences are likely to go on and on and on until you can think of a good way to finish. In other words you should always plan a-head.

3 Use short sentences.

4 Put each separate idea in a separate paragraph. Number each of the paragraphs if it will help the reader to understand better.

5 Use short words that everyone can understand.

6 Think about your reader. Your reader …

… must be able to see exactly what you mean:
your letters should be **CLEAR**

… must be given all the necessary information:
your letters should be **COMPLETE**

… is probably a busy person with no time to waste:
your letters should be **CONCISE**

… must be written in a sincere, polite tone:
your letters should be **COURTEOUS**

… should not be distracted by mistakes in grammar, punctuation or spelling:
your letters should be **CORRECT**

A dull or confusing layout makes a letter difficult to read.

2 *Work in groups* Compare the points you've highlighted. Then discuss these questions:

- Which of the ideas do you disagree with? Why?
- Which of the 'rules' (if any) don't apply to faxes and memos?
- If you receive a business letter, what impression do you get from these features:

A letter which is handwritten

A letter which has been printed on a dot matrix printer

A letter in large print

A letter printed in a decorative or unusual print

A letter printed on recycled paper

A letter with lots of very short paragraphs

A letter with very long paragraphs without any white space between them

A letter with numbered paragraphs

The design of the company's letterhead and the logo

A **1** *Work in pairs* Look at the letters on these pages and then discuss these questions:
  - Which of the two letters would you prefer to have received? Why?
  - What kind of impression does each letter give the reader?

2 **abc** Highlight the features which you think are most effective and put a wavy line under any parts which you dislike. Refer back to the 'Golden Rules' in **2.3C**.

SUNSHINE FLAVOURS LTD.

**44 Emerald Drive, Shannon Technology Park,
Cork CO6 9TS, Republic of Ireland.**

Mme Susanne Dufrais,
Les Gourmets du Poitou S.A.,
33, rue Mirabeau,
44000 Poitiers, France

18 January 1999

Dear Madam,

<u>Your request for our catalogue and price list</u>

   As requested, we enclose for your attention our price list and catalogue. I should like to take this opportunity of drawing your attention to the fact that all our products are manufactured from completely natural ingredients and that we do not utilize any artificial additives whatsoever.
   There are 213 different items in the catalogue and our prices are reasonable and our quality is good. This is the first time that we have included Scratch'n'Sniff™ samples of our ten most popular aromas.
   Should you require further information, please do not hesitate to contact us. If the undersigned is unavailable, the Sales Manager's personal assistant will be delighted to assist you.

   We look forward to receiving your esteemed order in due course.

Yours faithfully,

J.G. O'Reilly

J.G. O'Reilly, Sales Manager

**Telex: 449801   Telephone: 021 23 45 9
cables: SUNSHINE, CORK**

SUNSHINE FLAVOURS

44 Emerald Drive
Shannon Technology Park
Cork CO6 9TS
Republic of Ireland

Mme Susanne Dufrais
Les Gourmets du Poitou S.A.
33 rue Mirabeau
44000 Poitiers
France

18 January 1999

Dear Madame Dufrais,

You asked us to send you our price list and catalogue for the new season. I am sure you will find plenty to interest you in it. You will notice that every single one of our products is made from 100% natural ingredients – we use no artificial additives at all.

This year, for the very first time, we have included Scratch'n'Sniff™ samples of our ten most popular aromas. I think you will agree that our range of well over 200 natural flavours and aromas is second to none and is outstanding value for money.

If you need more information, do please get in touch with me. If you are telephoning, please ask to speak to me personally or to my assistant, Ms Hannah Rosser, and we will be very pleased to help you.

I look forward to hearing from you.

Yours sincerely,

Jim O'Reilly

James O'Reilly
Sales Manager

Enclosed: catalogue, price lists, order form

Telephone: 021 23 45 9
Fax: +353 21 23 44 7

B ◎◎ We asked eight business people this question:

What do you do before you write a difficult letter or a report?

Listen to what they said. Which of them do you agree with?

Work in groups Find out what methods your partners use when planning to write an important letter in their own language.

C Because writing a letter in English is much harder than writing one in your own language, careful planning is essential. Imagine, for example, you have to write a letter introducing your company to a prospective customer ...

ak▪ Highlight what you think are the most important points in this text and then compare your ideas with a partner.

Planning a Letter: 7 Steps

❶ Write down your AIM: what is the purpose of this letter?

❷ ASSEMBLE all the relevant information and documents: copies of previous correspondence, reports, figures, etc.

❸ ARRANGE the points in order of importance. Decide which points are irrelevant and can be left out. Make rough notes.

❹ Write an OUTLINE in note form. Check it through considering these questions:
  • Have you left any important points out?
  • Can the order of presentation be made clearer?
  • Have you included anything that is not relevant?

❺ Write a FIRST DRAFT, leaving plenty of space for changes and revisions.

❻ REVISE your first draft by considering these questions:
  • INFORMATION: Does it cover all the essential points?
    Is the information RELEVANT, CORRECT and COMPLETE?
  • ENGLISH: Are the grammar, spelling and punctuation correct?
  • STYLE: Does it look attractive?
    Does it sound natural and sincere?
    Is it CLEAR, CONCISE and COURTEOUS?
    Will it give the reader the right impression?
    Is it the kind of letter you would like to receive yourself?

❼ Write, type or dictate your FINAL VERSION.

D *Work in pairs* Here are three extracts from letters that break some rules.

❶ Decide what is wrong with each one and <u>underline</u> any mistakes or faults.

❷ Rewrite each extract in your own words.

```
I noticed your advertisment in the Daily Planet amd I would be
gratefull if you could sned me further infomration about your
products My company is considering subcontracting some of its
office services and I beleive that you may be able ot supply us
with a sutiable service, Looking forware to hearing form you.
Yours faithfully.
```

```
Thank you very much for your letter of 15 January, which we received
today. In answer to your enquiry we have pleasure in enclosing an
information pack, giving full details of our services. If you would
like any further information, do please contact me by phone or in
writing and I will be pleased to help. I hope that our services will
be of interest to you and I look forward to hearing from you.
Yours sincerely,
```

```
There are a number of queries that I would like to raise about
your products and I would be grateful if you could ask a
representative to get in touch with me with a view to discussing
these queries and hopefully placing an order if the queries are
satisfactorily answered.
```

2.5 Sending messages

 Work in pairs Look at this rather confusing memo. What makes it difficult to follow?

M E M O R A N D U M

TO: All members of staff, Northern Branch

FROM: KLJ

DATE: 2 December 1999

As you know, one of the reasons for the introduction of laptops in Northern Branch was to provide us with feedback before we decide whether to provide laptops for staff in other departments. The Board has asked me to submit a report on your experiences by the end of this week. I talked to some of you informally about this last month. During my brief visit I noticed a group of people in the canteen playing some kind of computer game and I heard from a senior manager that he only used his for <u>writing letters</u> — a job for a secretary, surely? So that I can compile a full report, I would like everyone to let me know what they personally use their laptop for, what software they use and how long per day they spend actually using it. It would also be useful to find out how their laptop has not come up to expectations, and any unexpected uses they have found for their laptop, so that others can benefit from your experience.

KLJ

➊ Decide how it can be improved.

➋ Redraft it together in your own words.

➌ Compare your version with the one in File **63** and with another pair's version.

B *Work in pairs or small groups* Imagine that you want to send Messages 1 to 5.

1 Decide what is the best way for each message to be transmitted:
- as a letter
- as a fax
- in a phone call
- in a face-to-face meeting

2 Plan and then draft the LETTERS and/or FAXES.

3 Another pair receives each letter and fax. They evaluate them according to the 'Golden Rules' in **2.3 C**.

4 Work with another pair Role-play the PHONE CALLS and/or face-to-face MEETINGS.

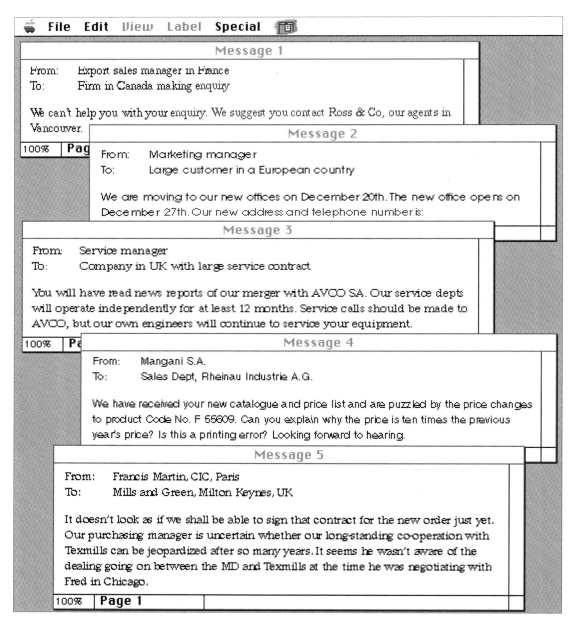

File   Edit   View   Label   Special

Message 1

From: Export sales manager in France
To: Firm in Canada making enquiry

We can't help you with your enquiry. We suggest you contact Ross & Co, our agents in Vancouver.

100%   Pag

Message 2

From: Marketing manager
To: Large customer in a European country

We are moving to our new offices on December 20th. The new office opens on December 27th. Our new address and telephone number is:

Message 3

From: Service manager
To: Company in UK with large service contract

You will have read news reports of our merger with AVCO SA. Our service depts will operate independently for at least 12 months. Service calls should be made to AVCO, but our own engineers will continue to service your equipment.

100%   Pa

Message 4

From: Mangani S.A.
To: Sales Dept, Rheinau Industrie A.G.

We have received your new catalogue and price list and are puzzled by the price changes to product Code No. F 55609. Can you explain why the price is ten times the previous year's price? Is this a printing error? Looking forward to hearing.

Message 5

From: Francis Martin, CIC, Paris
To: Mills and Green, Milton Keynes, UK

It doesn't look as if we shall be able to sign that contract for the new order just yet. Our purchasing manager is uncertain whether our long-standing co-operation with Texmills can be jeopardized after so many years. It seems he wasn't aware of the dealing going on between the MD and Texmills at the time he was negotiating with Fred in Chicago.

100%   Page 1

★★   REMEMBER: Whatever you're writing, always try to think about your reader's reaction.

3 On the phone

3.1 I'd like to speak to ...

A *Work in pairs* Look at the photos and discuss these questions:
- What's happening in each of the photos?
- What do you enjoy about using the phone?
- What do you dislike about making phone calls?

B Making a phone call to another company isn't always easy – especially if you don't know the person on the other end of the line very well …

❶ ◎◎ You'll hear Sylvia Perez trying to arrange an appointment with Dr Henderson, Head of Research at Richmond and Co. Ltd. As you listen, make a list of the things that went wrong:

✗ misunderstandings
✗ mistakes that the speakers made
✗ 'bad telephone style or behaviour'

❷ *Work in pairs* Compare your notes with a partner and discuss these questions:

- How did each of the misunderstandings happen?
- What *should* each of the people have done or said to avoid the problems and mistakes?

❸ *Work in groups* Compare your answers to the questions in **❷** with another pair's answers. Decide how *you* could avoid making the same mistakes as the speakers in the phone call.

C ◎◎ Now imagine that *you're* the one who's trying to get in touch with Dr Henderson. (His phone number is 0044 1234 32453.)

Decide what you would say in each situation … Dr Henderson is quite a hard man to find!

D ◎◎ ⏸ *Work in pairs* Listen to the recording and look at these phrases that are used when you're on the phone. Highlight the ones you find most useful.

> *Hello, I'd like to speak to Mr …*
> *Hello, this is Miss … calling from …*
> *Is Ms … available, please? My name's …*

> *Speaking.*
> *I'm afraid he's in a meeting / not in the office / still at lunch / not available just now. Is there anything I can do for you?*
> *Hold on a moment, please.*
> *I'll just find out if she's back yet / in the other office / available.*
> *I'll put you through to Miss …*
> *I'll ask her to call you back as soon as she's free.*
> *What's your extension number / fax number?*

> *Could you ask her to call me back, please? My number is …*
> *Could you give him a message, please?*
> *What time do you expect her back?*
> *I'll call again later today.*
> *Thanks very much for your help.*

E [icon] *Work in pairs* Follow this flowchart to practise making a phone call, using some of the expressions in **D**. Do this twice, so that you each have a turn playing both roles.

To simulate the situation of a telephone conversation, you and your partner must sit back-to-back like this:

– so that you can't see each other's faces.

A

Ask to speak to Mr Anderson.

B

> He's in a meeting.

Ask when he'll be free.

> You don't know. Offer to find out.

Say you'll wait.

> He won't be free till after 6 pm.

You want him to call you first thing tomorrow.

> Find out caller's name and number.

Give your (real) name and number.

> Note down the information and say you'll leave the message on his desk.

Say thanks and goodbye.

F *Work in small groups* Find out what your partners think about these questions:

- What is difficult about making a first-time call to a stranger?
- What can you do to make such calls easier?
- What can you do to establish a relationship with a stranger more quickly?
- How can you make sure that the other person knows who you are and what you want?
- If you have proposed an appointment or a meeting, how can you be sure that the other person has fully understood your intention?

"His phone is busy, his fax is busy, and his modem is busy. I'll just walk over and talk to him."

3.2 Getting people to do things

  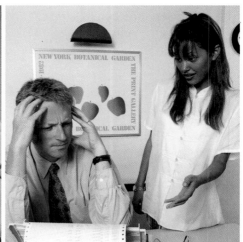

A *Work in pairs* Look at the pictures and discuss these questions:
- What's happening in each picture?
- What exactly are the people going to say to each other?
- Why is it important to sound and look polite when asking people to do something for you?

B ◎◎ *Work in pairs* Listen to the recording and follow the instructions below. After each step compare notes with your partner.

1 You'll hear two colleagues on the phone. Put a ☑ or ☒ to show if TERRY agrees or refuses to do these things for Jane.

send a copy of the report	☐
arrange accommodation	☐
call Sandy in New York	☐
translate a document into English	☐
check her punctuation and spelling	☐

2 **at** Listen to the conversation again and highlight the phrases they use:

Requesting

I'd like you to ... , please.
Could you ask ... to ... for me?
Could you ... , please?
Do you think you could ...?
Would you mind ...-ing ...?

Sure.
Certainly.
I won't be able to ... , because ...
I'm sorry but ...
I'm afraid that's not possible, because ...

---

③ You'll hear two more colleagues on the phone. Put a ☑ or ☒ to show if SALLY accepts or rejects each of Bill's offers to help.

check today's correspondence ☐
call a taxi for the airport ☐
check her hotel booking ☐
deal with the weekly report ☐
call Amsterdam ☐

④ 🔊 Listen to the conversation again and highlight the phrases they use:

Offering to help

> Can I give you a hand?
> Would you like a hand with ...?
> Shall I ...?
> Would you like me to ...?
> If you need any help, just let me know.

> Yes, please. Thanks a lot.
> No, thanks, I think I can manage.
> That's very kind of you, but ...
> I think I'd prefer to do that myself
>   because ...

⑤ You'll hear two people talking in an office. Put a ☑ or ☒ to show if the HOST gives his permission to the visitor to do these things:

open the window ☐
take off his jacket ☐
smoke ☐
use the phone to book a table for lunch ☐
call his office ☐
send a fax to Canada ☐

⑥ 🔊 Listen to the conversation again and highlight the phrases they use:

Asking permission

> May I ...?
> Do you mind if I ...?
> Could I ...?
> Is it all right if I ...?
> Do you think I could ...?

> Sure, go ahead.
> By all means.
> No, I'm afraid you can't, because ...
> I'm sorry but ...

★★ Remember that sounding polite and helpful doesn't just depend on the words you use, but also on the way you say them and (if you're talking to someone face-to-face) your body language.

C [icon] *Work in pairs* Imagine that one of you works for Europrint, a firm of package designers and printers, and the other for their customer, Utopia Products, a firm marketing consumer goods. You're going to role-play four short telephone conversations involving requests, offers and asking permission.

One of you should look at File **3**, the other at **34**.

To simulate the situation of a telephone conversation, you and your partner must sit back-to-back so that you can't see each other's faces.

[icon] Before you begin, look at these examples and listen to the recording:

> MESSAGE: **Request confirmation of receipt of samples, sent airmail on 6 February.**

> REPLY: **The first set hasn't arrived. Request further set of samples by courier.**

D *Work in pairs* Imagine that one of you is a foreign visitor to your country:
- Find out / explain how to make a call from a public telephone.
- Find out / explain what special telephone facilities and useful numbers a foreign visitor should know about.

3.3 Can I take a message?

A [icon] *Work in pairs* You'll hear a phone call. What improvements can you suggest to the way this message has been noted down?

Discuss these questions:
- What are the important points to consider when you have to take a message?
- If you answer the phone and have to take a message, what information do you note down, apart from the message itself?
- What do you do if an answering machine unexpectedly answers?

Mr Brown or Braun called about Tuesday. Wants you to call him back later.

B [icon] *Work in pairs* You'll hear three phone calls.

1 Listen to the calls and note down each message.

2 Compare the way you have written down the messages with the way your partner has.

1

To: *M. Février* **Date:** *4 Sept*
Message: *Mr Peter Schulz called from Vienna.*
Please call him before 4 pm . . .

2

To: **Date:** *September 4*
Message:

3

To: **Date:** *4th Sept*
Message:

C [image] It isn't always easy to understand people over the phone. You'll hear some orders being placed but each caller is talking quickly or unclearly. Listen carefully and work out what the callers are saying. Tick ☑ the information that is given.

300 kilos of white mice		300 kilos of white rice ✓
18 cents per kilo ✓		80 cents per kilo
2 boxes striped pyjamas		2 boxes ripe bananas
£115 per box		£150 per box
The total price is 4,295 francs.		The total price is 4,259 francs.
Our phone number is 456894.		Our phone number is 456984.
40 kilos @ £14 per kilo		14 kilos @ £40 per kilo
Order number: GJ 404		Order number: JG 404
900 items will cost $500		500 items will cost $900
Item code: RAE 77		Item code: AEI 77

➡ Compare your answers with a partner.

D [image] *Work in pairs* One of you should look at File **4**, the other at **35**. You will be taking part in two more telephone conversations, so sit back-to-back again.

❶ Make notes before you start each call.

❷ Role-play the calls.

❸ *Join another pair* Discuss these questions:
- Did the calls develop in the way you expected?
- What went wrong?   • What went right?

3.4 Planning and making calls

A ❶ [image] *Work in pairs* We asked eight business people this question:

How do you prepare for an important phone call?

Listen to their comments and decide which of their ideas you agree with.

❷ *Join another pair* Look again at **2.4❻**. Decide which of the '7 Steps' for planning a letter can be applied to preparing for an important phone call.

B *Work in groups* Read this extract from a training manual and then discuss the questions below:

Twelve telephone tips

1 Fax ahead if you want to make sure the other person has time to prepare for the call.

2 Make sure you have with you all the documents you'll need before you dial the number.

3 The other person may not understand you easily, so try to speak slowly and CLEARLY.

4 The other person can't see your reactions, so always CONFIRM that you have (or have not) understood each point that's been made. Don't pretend you have understood when you haven't.

5 The other person can't see what a nice person you are, so make sure you sound POLITE and AGREEABLE.

6 The other person hasn't got all day, so make sure your call is BRIEF.

7 The other person is getting an impression of your firm while talking with you, so make sure that you sound EFFICIENT – your firm's image may be at stake, even if you're just taking a message.

8 Don't rely on your memory: make notes during a call and rewrite these notes immediately afterwards as a record of the call.

9 Smile while you're talking. Your listener can 'hear' your smile.

10 Don't try to be funny – you may be misunderstood.

11 Don't interrupt the other person: let them finish what they want to say.

12 Send a follow-up fax or letter to confirm any important details (especially prices and numbers), so that you both have a written record of them.

- Which do you think are the five most important tips?
- Which of the tips do you disagree with? Why?
- Which of the advice do you already always follow when making or receiving a phone call in English?
- Which of the points do you feel *least* confident about if you're using English on the phone?
- What aspects of telephoning in English can be improved by more practice?

C 〔👥〕 *Work in groups of three (or four)* You will be taking it in turns to role-play a phone call. The third (and fourth) person will listen in and comment on your performance later.

To simulate the situation of a telephone conversation, the people on the phone must sit back-to-back so that you can't see each other's faces.

Student A should look at File **6**, student B at **37**, student C at **64** (and in a group of four, student D also at **64**). Follow the instructions in your File to find out what to do when the first call is finished. In all there are four different role-plays in the Files.

➡ Before you start, look again at the twelve tips in **B**.

(If you 'get lost' during these role-plays and don't know which File to look at next, ask your teacher for help.)

'Observer's' guidelines

When you're listening to your partners 'on the phone', think about these questions:
- Does each speaker sound agreeable, polite and efficient?
- Do they sound natural and sincere?
- Does each speaker's tone create the right impression?
- Are they speaking clearly?
- Is the information they're giving correct?
- Have they both covered all the essential points?
- Is it the kind of call you would like to receive yourself?

➡ Comment on the call by giving 'feedback' to the two speakers.

D *Work in groups* Discuss these questions with your partners:
- Which parts of the role-plays in **C** did you find most difficult?
- How did your performance improve as you got more practice?

4 Summaries, notes, reports

4.1 Summarizing a conversation

🄐 *Work in groups* Imagine these pictures show your office. Discuss these questions:
- What seems to be going on in each picture? (Identify the kinds of communication going on.)
- How much communication do *you* do by speaking to people and how much by writing to people?
- What are some of the advantages of communicating in writing, rather than relying on the spoken word?

⚠️ It's important to take notes on business conversations, rather than rely on your memory. The main points need to be clearly recorded so that another person can make sense of them – and you have a permanent record for the files.

B  *Work in pairs* You'll hear a conversation recorded at a trade exhibition. Listen to the recording of the meeting between two people and decide which of these three styles of summary you prefer.

ROTAPLEX plc   Fount Lane Cowdray Norfolk CW3 7UJ

1 July 1999

During my duty period on the company stand, I was approached by a man called Tim Brown. He enquired about our rotary printer. It was the R75 he was interested in. In particular, he asked whether the machine was able to deal with

Notes on the Proprinta Exhibition
To:
From: TR Sales Manager (Tim Raven)
Subject: BN (Bob Norman) Sales Representative
Firm: Record of consultation at PROPRINTA 30.6.99
Person met: Happy Greeting Cards
Nature of enquiry: Tim Brown, Procurement
   About R75

RECORD OF CONVERSATION AT PROPRINTA
Date 30.6.99
1 Met Brown from Happy Greeting Cards
2 He expressed interest in 10 R75s
3 They want 15% discount on large order
4 He says PRINTIX Inc. will give him 15%

C   Listen to the recording again.

1 Now draft a summary of the conversation in your own words.

2 *Work in pairs* Compare your summary with your partner's. Have you both noted down ALL the important information? Have you noted down any *un*necessary information?

"Everything I turned my hand to was a disaster until I started a School of Business Management."

A *Work in pairs* Imagine that your managing director has asked you to investigate the health and safety provisions in your company's offices and to make recommendations for improvement.

These are the notes that you've made. Draft a report to your MD by expanding the notes into paragraphs.

Health and safety issues considered during past year

Studied all reports of job-related illnesses, e.g. colds and 'office bugs'.
A number of cases of symptoms of Repetitive Strain Injury (RSI) reported by company physiotherapist.
Had meetings with union reps and office managers about what to do.

Recommendations / Proposals

1 Clearly display safety regulations in canteen and main offices.
2 New staff need informing about safety regulations and policy, e.g. on taking frequent breaks from the screen.
3 Office staff need training on how to position themselves, their chairs, desks and equipment.
4 Departmental committee on health and safety to be responsible for instructing new staff on procedures for handling office equipment and for securing electronic / mechanical machinery.
5 Ventilation and air-filtering systems in offices need regular maintenance.
6 Union suggested replacement of sub-standard furniture and equipment, especially:
   a old-fashioned screens — cause eyesight problems
   b carefully check office lighting — staff complaints of headaches after work / lighting large part of problem; bright lights should not reflect on the screen
   c essential to have chairs with full back supports — many staff complaints of backache

---

➡ Begin your report like this:

```
To:      Ms Renoir, Managing Director
From:    (your name)              Date:


Office health and safety provisions


As requested by the Managing Director on 30 March
1999, I have investigated the problems which have been
raised concerning office health and safety.
```

B *Join another pair* Compare your draft reports.

➡ Look at File **67** for a suggested draft. Compare your own reports with it. What differences are there between your reports and the one in File **67**?

4.3 Planning and editing a report

A *Work in pairs*
Here are some of the tasks that may be involved in writing a report.

If you were writing a report, which order would you do the tasks in? Number the items, *leaving out* any points you think are unimportant.

Consider the purpose of your report: who is it for, why does he/she want it, how will he/she use it?
Draft a working plan on a separate sheet of paper.
Write the body of the report.
Write the introduction: state the subject, state the purpose, summarize your findings.
State the aim and emphasis of the report briefly.
Collect all relevant material – notes, documents, etc.
Check your grammar, spelling, punctuation and style.
Read the text aloud to yourself, or, better, to someone else.
Decide what information is important and what is irrelevant.
Arrange the points of information in a logical sequence and in order of importance. Make rough notes.
Finally, if possible, let someone qualified to give constructive criticism look at your draft.
Decide where you might need illustrations or diagrams.
Write the conclusion (and recommendations).
Check your illustrations.
Summarize the report in a sentence.
Examine the draft. Does it do what the report is expected to do?

➡ Have any other important points been left out which you think should be included?

B *Work in groups* Now discuss the order you decided on and the reasons why. What areas do you agree and disagree about?

⚠ It's important in any writing and – especially in business – to be clear about the aims and purposes of your writing.
To help your reader to make sense of what you've written:

    be **ACCURATE**   be **BRIEF**   be **CLEAR**   be **DECISIVE**

C *Work in pairs* Read the following memo and imagine that you are a Divisional Personnel Manager to whom the memo is addressed. Then discuss these questions:
- What do you think the Managing Director's aims were in writing the memo?
- What – if anything – are you expected to do as a result of reading the memo?

MEMORANDUM

From: The Managing Director   **To:** Divisional Personnel Managers
Subject: Clocking-in Machines   **Date:** 27/4/99

There have been a number of comments about the amount of time being wasted with extended lunch breaks in our company. I do not want to sound as though I am against breaks, in principle; indeed our personnel consultants have emphasized how important and efficiency-promoting such regular interruptions can be if you want an effective and motivated office staff. But, we must keep a check on working hours and clocking-in machines for office staff do exist. We can expect a little opposition to the idea if we are not careful. You can never be sure how the office staff will react. They might well take it badly. In any case, we're thinking of putting in clocking-in machines for all clerical grades; please send me a report.

D *Work in pairs* Now look at this report, which was written *after* receiving the memo from the MD and discuss these questions:

- Do you think the report is what the MD asked for?
- How effective do you think the report is?

at© Highlight the things you find good in it and <u>underline</u> the things you think are bad.

6/5/99

REPORT ON CLOCKING-IN MACHINES AND TIME-KEEPING

It is very interesting that the time-keeping habits of our employees have been noticed by other people in the company. It appears as if the time lost by extended use of lunch breaks could be avoided. We have also known for some time that there have been a number of problems connected with the motivation of our workforce, but the role played by the apparently informal extension of lunch breaks has so far not been clarified.

In one or two departments, reports of staff taking extended breaks and long lunch hours without a colleague to cover them are well known. This unfortunate development has been discussed with the heads of department in my division on several occasions. They believe the subject of clocking-in machines, one for each department for example, is not very popular with a large number of staff. The staff think that the company does not respect the majority of the staff's honesty and that the company is thinking in narrow money terms, which are not worthy of salaried employees. So I think that there is a grave danger that the actions of the management could be misunderstood.

Nonetheless, I feel that we should try and limit the advantages that certain individuals are taking with time-keeping. We should undertake a review of selected staff. I wonder if you have heard of the experience of our American sister company? They have a central clocking-in system for all the divisional offices. As soon as employees switch on their terminals at the start of the day this is easily checked on the main computer. In this way there is always a clear record of how many extra hours of overtime have been worked. This is a great help for some members of staff in planning their holiday requests. In theory this is surely one way of making working time more efficient.

E *Work in pairs* You probably agree that the Managing Director didn't make his or her intentions clear enough in the memo. To write a clear report you need a clear aim to start with. The kind of report you write depends on how you interpret the memo.

❶ Look at File **69** for a clearer specification of what the MD really wanted.

❷ Draft a report with your partner.

❸ *Join another pair* Compare your report with the one above *and* the other pair's report.

"Damn it, Brookner, it seems to me your time could be better spent than by consolidating all your little notes to yourself into one big neat one."

4.4 Making notes

A *Work in pairs* Look at these tips on making notes. Discuss these questions:
- Which of the advice do you already follow?
- Which is the most important tip, as far as you're concerned?
- Which tip is the most *helpful* and the most *unhelpful*?

1 It's not a good idea to write your notes in complete sentences. Keep notes short.

2 Use abbreviations. But not so many that you can't understand your own notes later!

3 Use words like **because**, **therefore**, **but**, or **and** to show how ideas are related.

4 Use the dash – . It's a very useful punctuation mark in note-making.

5 Use a lot of space   – then you can e x p a n d your notes later. Put each separate idea on a new line.

6 Use the layout to help make the meaning clear. Use new paragraphs, **headings**, CAPITAL LETTERS and <u>underlinings</u>.

B ◎◎ *Work in pairs* You'll hear three short conversations. Look at these notes, which were made in different styles, as you listen to the conversations.

Some of the points in the notes are not in the correct order – rearrange them as necessary.

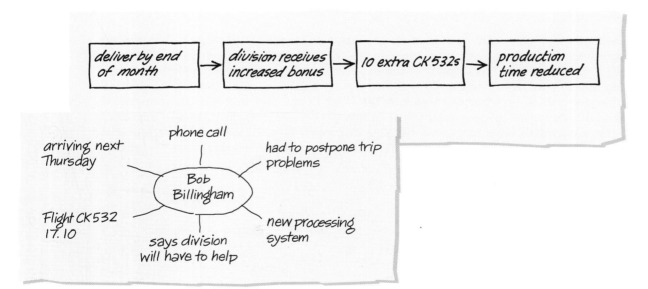

➡ Which of the three methods of making notes do you prefer?

C *Work in pairs* Using the notes in **B**, take it in turns to tell each other what each conversation was about.

Unit 4 Summaries, notes, reports

D  🔊 You'll hear a lecturer describing a method of making notes.

❶ Take notes. (If you wish, you can use one of the methods shown opposite.)

❷ *Work in pairs* Compare your notes with a partner's notes. Then draft a summary of what the person says.

❸ *Work in groups* Look at your partners' summaries and then discuss these questions:

- What do you find difficult about making notes?
- Why is it important to make notes, rather than rely on your memory?
- Do you use a different method of making notes which works well? Tell your partners about it.
- Which method of making notes do you prefer? Why?

4.5 Punctuation

A *Work in pairs* Match these punctuation marks to their names below. (The first is a *comma*.)

, ! "..." / (...) ? ' '...' ; : . - —

*apostrophe   brackets / parentheses   colon   comma   dash   exclamation mark
full stop / period   hyphen   question mark   semi-colon   single quotes
stroke / oblique / slash   double quotes / quotation marks / inverted commas*

B *Work in pairs* Complete these sentences by deciding which punctuation mark is 'explained' or 'illustrated'.

1 The words 'explained' or 'illustrated' in this sentence are between `single quotes` .
2 A   marks the end of a sentence.
3 A   shows that there is some doubt, doesn't it? What do you think?
4 A   is used for word-division or word-joining.
5 And it should not be confused with another – longer – mark: the
   This is used to separate ideas or words – usually added as an afterthought.
6 When writers wish to express emphasis or even surprise they use the
                          . This is no problem!
7 "   are used to show what someone actually said."
8 Sometimes you may wish to separate two sentences; but they are somehow closely connected; this is when you can use the   instead of the full stop.
9 NOTE: a   can help to emphasize what is coming next: to list things: reports, letters, memos and so on.
10 If a person wants to show alternatives, he/she can separate them by using a
                  /   /   .
11 And if they are using words (i.e. phrases or expressions) which are not of primary importance they can be placed between   (   ).
12 An   is used in possessives (Mr Jones's) and it's also used in contractions, isn't it?

C *Work in pairs* Find the errors in these sentences and correct them.

1 Its important, that your punctuation is correct: because incorrect punctuation and Capital Letters Used Wrongly may confuse your readers'

2 Just like, incorrect spelling incorrect punctuation can be very annoying for your reader who may pay more attention to `the mistakes, than to the content of your report or letter.

3 You probably know, that exclamation marks are not used much in business letters! But they are used in advertisements as well as in notes.

4 Contracted forms like Ive and weve are a feature of informal writing. They are not found in most reports or business letters which tend to be fairly formal. If in doubt use the full forms; I have, we have, etc

5 It's usually easier for a reader to understand short simple sentences rather than long complicated one's.

D *Work in pairs* Look at the following text and decide where to add punctuation. You'll also need to add line breaks (new paragraphs) and some Capital Letters.

memo from the managing director to all office staff date 25th november 1999 as a result of the productivity survey carried out in the factory more rapid and efficient ways of operating are now being applied in the factory productivity has been increased by over 50 per cent the management intends to apply these same methods to office staff in order to reduce costs our company must adapt in a competitive world we aim to find ways of avoiding unnecessary actions by all staff we therefore propose to pay a months extra salary to any person who in the managements opinion has put forward the most practical suggestion to improve a particular office routine all suggestions should be sent to the mds office before the end of next month

"You know Miss Fishgrove, comma, or may I call you Mary, question mark, I've often ..."

5 Working together

5.1 Getting to know the workplace ...

A ◎◎ *Work in pairs* You'll hear a new employee being told where the different offices are in the firm he has just joined.

Listen to the conversation and number the rooms that Michael is shown. The 'tour' starts at Mrs Bronson's office.

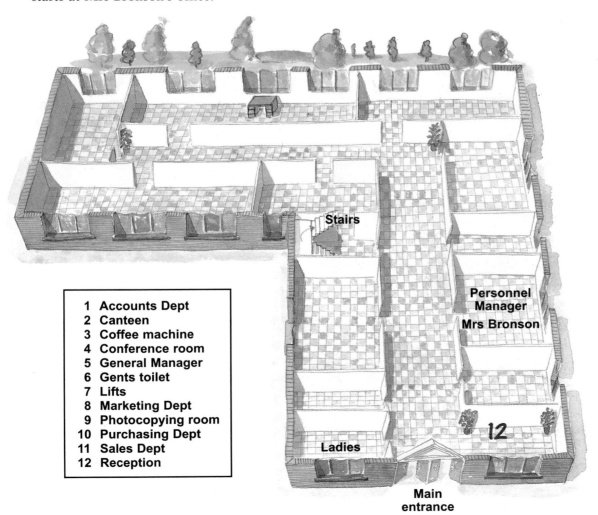

1 Accounts Dept
2 Canteen
3 Coffee machine
4 Conference room
5 General Manager
6 Gents toilet
7 Lifts
8 Marketing Dept
9 Photocopying room
10 Purchasing Dept
11 Sales Dept
12 Reception

B *Work in pairs* Imagine that a friend is about to start a new job. Decide which are the SIX most important pieces of advice that you'd give to your friend for their first day at work. Which of these tips do you disagree with?

- ☑ Arrive twenty minutes early.
- ☑ Wear your smartest clothes (not trousers if you're a woman).
- ☐ Go to the hairdresser's the day before.
- ☐ Smile at everybody you meet.
- ☑ Make a note of everything anyone tells you.
- ☐ Show your new colleagues pictures of your family.

- ☑ If you're a smoker, don't smoke in an office you share with someone.
- ☐ If you're a non-smoker and the person you share the office with is a smoker, say you don't mind if they smoke.
- ☐ Enquire about the company pension scheme.
- ☐ Ask who the trade union representative is.

➡ If you think any of them are 'silly' pieces of advice, how would you change them? Add two more pieces of advice you'd give to someone starting a new job.

C *Work in pairs* Office life is different from country to country. What would you tell a foreign visitor about office routines in your country?

working hours
union recognition
recreational and sports facilities for staff

child-care facilities
relationships between boss and employees
holidays

D *Work in pairs* Imagine that an important visitor is coming to your firm. She has sent you this fax. Before you reply to it in ❹, go through steps ❶ to ❸.

TIVOLI DESIGN CONSORTIUM

BERSTORFFSGADE 19, DK-1577 COPENHAGEN, DENMARK
TELEPHONE: +(45) 72 14 33 21   FAX: +(45) 56 39 42 38

TO: Publicity Office / Manager

Dear Sir or Madam,

We have heard from one of our mutual customers that your company is involved in a number of interesting design projects.

As I am shortly staying in your city on business, I am writing to enquire whether it would be convenient to visit your office.

I shall be in town from 14th to 18th November. I would be free any morning from 11.30 onwards and in the afternoon of 15th November.

I would be extremely grateful if you could confirm whether a brief visit could be arranged on one of the days and at the times suggested.

I look forward to hearing from you.

Yours faithfully,

Anita Trosborg

Design Director

1 Decide what people and which areas you will show Ms Trosborg round.

2 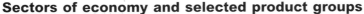 Make a telephone call to a colleague in another department, enquiring whether you can bring Ms Trosborg to see him/her. One of you should look at File **9** and the other at File **39**.

3 Write a memo asking your boss to give Ms Trosborg a brief explanation of your firm's activities.

4 Draft a fax to Ms Trosborg arranging the date and the time you propose for the visit, or if you prefer, phone her.

5.2 Different kinds of companies

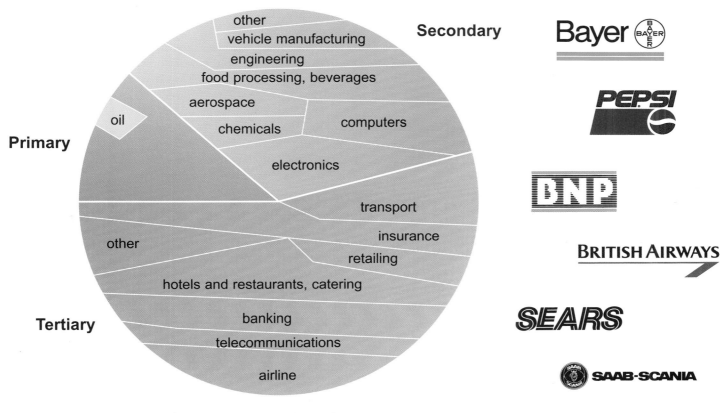

Sectors of economy and selected product groups

A *Work in groups* Which of these companies do you know? Match them up with the sectors of industry and the product groups in the chart. Discuss these questions:

- Which are the five largest or most important companies in your region (or country)?
- Which sectors of industry or product groups do they belong to?
- Make a list of the products they make or the services they supply.

➡ Compare your lists with another group.

B **1** *Work in pairs* Now read through this extract from a business textbook, which deals with a related topic. Fill each gap with one of these words.

another   basic   business   countries   economic   fishing   fully   labour   major   most   per cent   primary   productive   secondary   services   work   workers

Divisions of economic activity Although the structure of each country is different, their economies can be shown to have similar sectors. When speaking of _____ or economic activity, commentators normally recognize three 'sectors':

● primary – agriculture, fishing, mining, construction
● _____ – crafts and manufacturing
● tertiary – _____ , including education, banking, insurance, etc.

The occupational structure The types of activities that most _____ are occupied in differ, sometimes dramatically, from one country to _____ and from one time to another. In _____ developing countries (and in all _____ before the 19th century), the vast majority of the workforce _____ in the agricultural, or _____ , sector. Their work is almost entirely manual, and most of the country's _____ power is concentrated on the _____ task of feeding the population. In _____ developed countries far more of their _____ resources are directed towards other _____ activities. In the United States and Canada, for example, only 4 and 7 per cent, respectively, of all employed persons work in agriculture, _____ , and mining, compared to more than 70 _____ in India.

2 *Work in groups* Discuss these more general questions:
• What percentage of people working, approximately, are engaged in each of the sectors in your country?
• Which sector is contracting? Which is growing? Which is staying the same?
• In which sector are the most companies, businesses or enterprises in your region located, would you say?
• Which sector do you (or do you expect to) work in?
• Which areas of the economy in your country are changing most?
• Which areas have the most people working in them?
• Which areas are the most important?
• Which sectors can we not do without?

"We're a parent company, Wolper – not to be confused with your real parents."

SCHWADRON

5.3 Company organization

A ① *Work in pairs* Look at the structure of the company in the diagram. Guess what some of the missing job titles might be.

② Listen to the recording and fill in the names and titles or job descriptions that are missing.

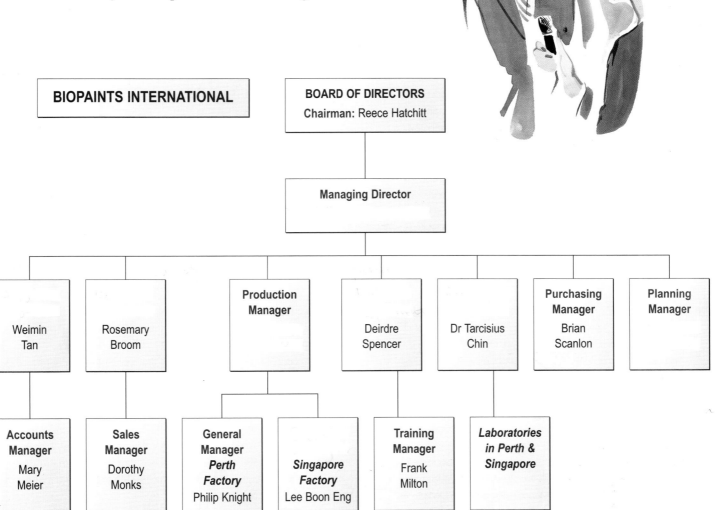

BIOPAINTS INTERNATIONAL

BOARD OF DIRECTORS
Chairman: Reece Hatchitt

Managing Director

Weimin Tan

Rosemary Broom

Production Manager

Deirdre Spencer

Dr Tarcisius Chin

Purchasing Manager
Brian Scanlon

Planning Manager

Accounts Manager
Mary Meier

Sales Manager
Dorothy Monks

General Manager
Perth Factory
Philip Knight

Singapore Factory
Lee Boon Eng

Training Manager
Frank Milton

Laboratories in Perth & Singapore

➡ Which of the people mentioned are also members of the board?

B *Work in pairs* Discuss with your partner what other parts of the company have perhaps not been mentioned.

To whom would the following people report?

the Public Relations Manager   the Works Manager
the Advertising Manager   the Export Manager   the Project Manager

➡ What companies do you know which are organized like Biopaints International?

C *Work in pairs* One of you should look at File **11** and the other at **43**. You'll each have different information about a company.

Ask questions to find out what your partner knows about the company.

A *Work in pairs* Look at the following passages about two companies.

1 Decide which of the headlines goes with which passage.

Planning and Building for over 150 years

Pioneering Tomorrow's Electronics

OVER THE DECADES, the name of Siemens has become synonymous with progress. Since 1847, when Werner Siemens and Johann Georg Halske founded the Siemens & Halske Telegraph Construction Company in Berlin, the history of Siemens has been closely linked with the development of electrical engineering. While still a fledgling firm, Siemens & Halske spearheaded the evolution of telegraphy with the first pointer telegraph and the construction of an extensive telegraph network. In 1866 Werner Siemens invented the dynamo machine, laying the cornerstone of power engineering.

New ideas are an old tradition at Siemens. The company that grew out of the original Siemens & Halske is today a highly innovative leader in the world electrical and electronics market. Composed of Siemens AG and an array of domestic and foreign subsidiaries, the contemporary Siemens organization continues to set milestones on the road of progress.

Siemens maintains its own production facilities in more than 50 countries and operates a worldwide sales network. With more than 300,000 employees, it is one of the largest companies in the world electrical/electronics industry, having recorded annual sales of DM 82 billion in the 1992/93 fiscal year. Reliable and farsighted management is united with the youthful dynamism and zest for innovation that typify the company.

IN 1849, JOHANN PHILIPP HOLZMANN founded a company in Sprendlingen, near Frankfurt am Main, which initially undertook work in connection with the construction of the railroads, but very quickly expanded its activities to include all fields of building construction and civil engineering. The first major foreign project was started in 1882, with the contract for Amsterdam's Central Station.

By the turn of the century, branch offices and regional offices had been established at numerous locations throughout Germany. As early as 1885, Holzmann had more than 5,000 employees. Interesting activities from this period include the company's work on the Baghdad railroad and railroad projects in East Africa.

Holzmann has passed through all forms of company organization, from individual proprietorship via a limited and general partnership through to a GmbH (limited liability company). The Philipp Holzmann Aktiengesellschaft (public limited company) was formed in 1917. Companies founded by Holzmann were active in South America.

Even following the losses of manpower and assets during the Second World War, Holzmann was able, as early as 1950, to recommence its foreign activities. 1979 saw the acquisition of J. A. Jones Construction Company, of Charlotte, North Carolina, USA, a major American corporation active in the construction field. This was followed in 1981 by the purchase of Lockwood Greene Engineers, Inc., Spartanburg, South Carolina, USA. Together with its USA subsidiaries Holzmann has responded to the changes occurring in the construction industry with a flexible and versatile corporate strategy.

The takeover in early 1989 of the Steinmüller Group, one of Germany's leading companies in the sectors of power engineering, process engineering and environmental protection demonstrates this.

2 Complete the information missing in this table:

Dates	What happened?	Who did what?
1847		
1849		
	Invention of dynamo machine	
	First large foreign order begun	

1885	
	Aktiengesellschaft founded
1950	
	Acquisition of J. A. Jones Construction Company
1981	
1989	
	Recorded annual sales of DM 82 billion

3 Complete the following table with information from the articles:

	HOLZMANN	SIEMENS
Locations of the company's activities		
Activities of both companies up to 1940s		
Recent activities of the companies		

B *Work in pairs* Imagine that you work in a company's publicity office or public relations department. An American company has written asking for some information about your company. Draft a short letter briefly summarizing the background, history and experience of your company.

If you don't work in a company, you may find it helpful to look at File **70** and imagine that you work for the company in the advertisement. Or write about a local company you know about.

1 Begin your letter like this:

```
Dear ...

You asked for some information about our company.
```

2 Try to answer some of these questions in the main body of the letter:
- What area or areas does the company work in?
- When did the company start?
- What products does the company manufacture?
- What recent activities of the company are worth mentioning?
- Where is the company located?
- How is the company structured?
- How many people are there on the workforce?
- How do you see the future of the company developing?
- Has much changed in the company in the past?

3 Finish your letter like this:

```
If you have any further questions, please get in touch with me.

Yours sincerely,
```

➡ When you've finished, compare your letter with another pair.

5.5 Working with others

I have yet to see a democratic workplace . . . People are treated like numbers . . .

Ricardo Semler

1 *Work in pairs* Read the following extracts from an article about a Brazilian company and choose one of these titles for it:

The World's Most Unusual Workplace
Different Types of Company Organization

Reorganizing Factory Work
Workers' Control Can Work

2 Find the answers to the following questions in the first extract:

1 Who makes the decisions?
2 What things have been abandoned?
3 How are salaries decided?
4 How are profits shared?
5 Who reorganizes the factories?

6 Who chooses new sites for development?
7 What role do computers play in the factory?
8 Who controls expenses and business travel?
9 Who makes the boss's tea?

Workers come and go as they please. They make vital decisions previously made by the bosses. Secretaries have been abolished (and given more rewarding jobs). The assembly line has been abandoned, as have economies of scale like buying components in bulk. A quarter of employees fix their own salaries and soon everyone will. The workers decide how much of the profits to share and how much to invest. Many of the rest are encouraged to work from home or set up their own small companies. Employees reorganize their factories and choose new sites for development. Central computers have been consigned to oblivion along with rows of unnecessary filing cabinets. Memos must be confined to one page. There are no controls over expenses or business travel. There is a reception desk, but no receptionist. The boss doesn't even have his own desk and has to make his own tea.

The company, Semco, located in São Paulo, Brazil, makes pumps, dishwashers and cooling units. It has been crawled over by the media and hundreds of curious corporations including 150 of the Fortune top 500 companies in the US. Semco has increased profits fivefold to nearly $3 million on sales approaching $30 million (after allowing for inflation despite the hyper-inflationary background of the national economy). It exports 23 per cent of output. Productivity has risen sevenfold and the company is free of debt.

3 Answer these questions:

1 What products does the company make?
2 How have the profits of Semco developed recently?
3 What is the sales situation?
4 What happens to its output?
5 How would you describe Semco's financial situation?

B ◎◎ You'll hear a radio discussion in which a business consultant, Robert, and an industrial correspondent, Jane, are asked by the radio programme host what they think about the company.

1 Listen to the recording for the first time and tick which of the following general topics are mentioned:

> bureaucracy at work
> staff promotion systems
> management elections by the workers
> the design of Semco's factory buildings
> the success of large corporations

2 ◎◎ Listen carefully for a second time and mark whether the statements below are true ☑ or false ☒:

1 The industrial assembly line system has a further 100 years' life in it. ☐
2 Democratic values of public life are limited in some countries. ☐
3 Managers are evaluated by their employees. ☐
4 Managers from outside the company are always welcome. ☐
5 Employees have developed a sense of responsibility. ☐
6 The associates just walk around the factory doing what they like. ☐
7 Many companies have not survived the high inflationary period. ☐
8 IBM has not been able to control the information flow in the company. ☐
9 Hundreds of companies have been following Semco's example. ☐
10 Corporate executives are eager to try out new ideas. ☐

I'll say this for him – he treats his staff just like they were his own children

C **❶** *Work in small groups* Ask the other members of your group what they think of these opinions about how work is organized. Decide which of the points you can agree on.

1 People working in business should be told what to do and should do it without asking questions.
2 Employees want to be recognized as people with their own (personal) needs.
3 Employees have to be forced to work: otherwise they are just lazy.
4 Managers need to closely control what employees do.
5 Nobody wants responsibility at work.
6 If there are problems to be solved, everybody should be asked their opinion before anything is done.

➡ You may find some of these expressions useful.

Agreeing and disagreeing

If you want to agree with someone you can say:

That's exactly what I think.
That's a good point.
Quite right, I couldn't agree more.

That's just what I was thinking.
I agree entirely.
Yes, I'm all in favour of that.

It's often considered rude or aggressive to say 'You're wrong' or 'I don't agree with you'. It's more polite to disagree with someone by saying:

I see what you mean, but ...
I don't think it's such a good idea ...
That's true, but on the other hand ...
I don't quite agree because ...
Maybe, but don't you think ...?

❷ *Join another group* Ask the other group what they have agreed on. Then discuss these questions:

• How authoritarian or co-operative should managers be?
• How democratic should the workplace be?

5.6 Women's work

A *Work in pairs* Think about the types of jobs people have in your country.

Make two lists:

PRESENT JOBS: jobs which many women now do, but which their mothers did not do in the past
PAST JOBS: jobs which their mothers' generation used to do, but which few women do now

And note down three REASONS why you think the changes have taken place.

Present jobs   Past jobs

Reasons for changes

1

2

3

B *Work in groups* Compare your lists and reasons with another pair. Then discuss these questions:

- Do you agree on the reasons why the changes have taken place?
- What sort of changes have taken place in the relationships between men and women at work?
- What further changes do you expect and would like to see?
- How have working conditions for women improved recently?
- How do they still need to be improved further?

C *Work in groups* Look at the cartoon strip and then discuss these questions:

What would it be like …

… if all the bosses in your place of work were women?
… if all the secretaries were men?
… if all the manual workers in your firm were women?
… if all the receptionists were men?

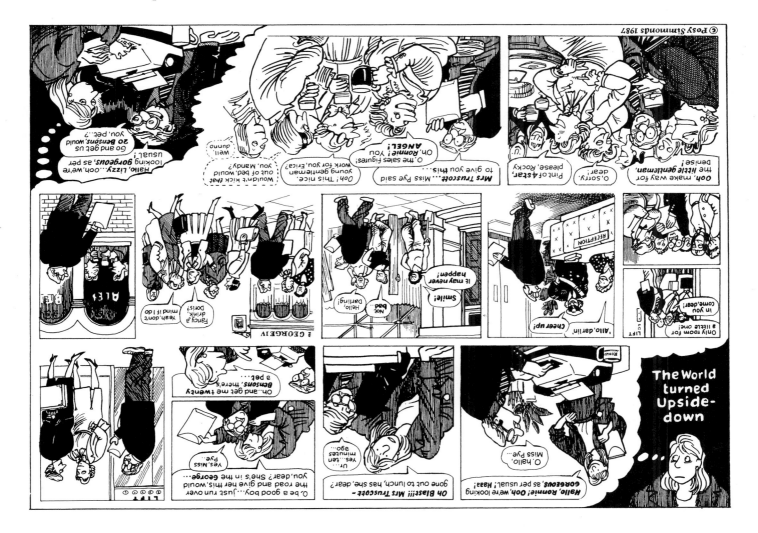

6 International trade

6.1 Exchanging information

A ◎◎ In the recording a customer, Mr Rusconi, and a supplier, Mr Garcia, are talking on the phone. You'll hear TWO versions of this conversation. Decide which of these words describe the IMPRESSION the two men give in each version of the conversation.

friendly informal helpful aggressive formal hostile polite impatient

➡ Listen to the two phone calls again. How does each speaker make himself sound more friendly and helpful in the second call?

B ◙◙ *Work alone* Highlight the expressions that you think are most useful. What other similar expressions can you add to each balloon?

If you require some information you can say:

> *Could you tell me if / when / how much / why ...?*
> *I wonder if you could tell me ...?*
> *I'd like to know ...*
> *I'd like some information about ...*

Or you can write:

```
We require the following information ...
Please let us know whether/when/how much ...
```

When someone gives you some information
you can comment or reply:

> Oh, I see.
> That's interesting.
> Thanks for letting me know.

If someone asks you for information you can reply:

> As far as I know, ...
> Well, (in confidence,) I can tell you that ...
>
> I'm afraid I don't know.
> I've no idea, I'm afraid.
> I don't have that information available just now, can I call you back?
> I'm not sure, I'll have to find out. Can I let you know tomorrow?
> I'm afraid I can't tell you that, it's confidential.

If you want to give someone some
information you can say:

> I'd like you to know that ...
> I think you should know that ...
> Did you know that ...?

Or you can write:

```
We should like to inform you that ...
Here is the information you requested ...
```

If someone hasn't given you enough information you can say:

> Could you tell me some more about ...?
> I'd like some more information about ...
> I'd also like to know ...
> When / How much / Why exactly ...?
> There's something else I'd like to know ...
> Can you give me some more details about ...?

C 　 *Work in pairs* One of you should look at File **12**, the other at **44**. Imagine that you're on the phone. You each have a copy of the same price list – but both copies are partially illegible! You'll need to ask questions to find out the missing information. Before you make the call, look again at the phrases above.

Imagine that you work for the same company, but you don't know each other well. So you should speak politely to each other.

D When you're giving someone an important piece of information, it's best to follow this rule: 'Speak clearly and slowly'.

◎◎ Unfortunately other people may not follow this rule! You'll hear various people asking for information – and all of them speak unclearly or quickly. Decide what each person wants to know and choose the correct alternative below.

1 The first person wants to know if the check-in time of the flight is …
   4.15 ☐   4.50 ☑   4.55 ☐

2 The second person wants to leave a message for …
   Mr Geoffrey ☑   Mr Geoffreys ☐   Mr Jeffrey ☐   Mr Jeffreys ☐

3 The third person wants to book some theatre tickets. He wants …
   2 seats on July 3rd ☑   3 seats on July 2nd ☐   2 seats on July 2nd ☐
   3 seats on July 3rd ☐

4 The fourth person wants to know if she can change to …
   a double room from the 29th ☑   a single room from the 29th ☐
   a single room from Friday ☐

5 The fifth person wants you to tell his agent in Greece to call him on …
   23983 before 3 ☑   28393 after 3.30 ☐
   29383 before 3 ☐   23893 after 3.30 ☐
   TWO of these four answers are correct!

6 The sixth person wants to know if there is …
   a party for delegates at the conference ☐
   a cheap party rate for delegates at a conference ☑

7 The seventh person wants to know …
   Mr Wilson's room number ☐   if Mr Wilson is in room 405 ☐
   if Mr Wilson will be back at 4.05 ☐
   if Mr Wilson left the hotel at 4.05 ☐

8 The eighth person wants to know how long it takes to get to the airport …
   by car ☐   by train ☐   by taxi ☐

E *Work in groups* Find out about the international business of the firms your partners work for (or firms they have worked for in the past, or in their work experience):
- How much of the company's business is with foreign countries?
- What proportion of their suppliers are foreign?
- What proportion of their customers are foreign?
- If these proportions are different, why is this so?
- Why is trade with foreign companies more difficult than trade with domestic companies?

"Mr Pointman, while you were out, a Miss or a Ms or a Mrs Valdy or Volney or Balmey left a garbled message for you."

Your role

Work in pairs You and your partner have just joined the Buying Department of BROADWAY AUTOS. Read this information about the company:

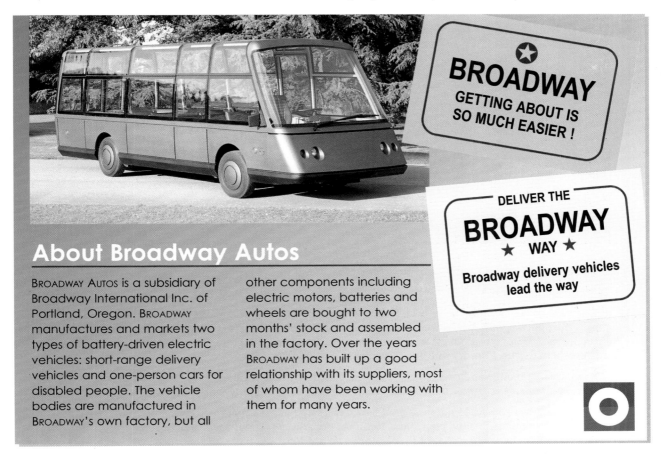

BROADWAY
GETTING ABOUT IS
SO MUCH EASIER !

DELIVER THE
BROADWAY
★ WAY ★
Broadway delivery vehicles
lead the way

About Broadway Autos

BROADWAY AUTOS is a subsidiary of Broadway International Inc. of Portland, Oregon. BROADWAY manufactures and markets two types of battery-driven electric vehicles: short-range delivery vehicles and one-person cars for disabled people. The vehicle bodies are manufactured in BROADWAY's own factory, but all other components including electric motors, batteries and wheels are bought to two months' stock and assembled in the factory. Over the years BROADWAY has built up a good relationship with its suppliers, most of whom have been working with them for many years.

A ① 〇〇 Listen to Fred North, your boss, talking on the phone. Make notes on the call. Compare your notes with your partner's.

② While Mr North is at lunch you notice this article in today's paper. Decide together what you will say to Mr North when he gets back from lunch.

Arcolite to close Winterthur factory

ARCOLITE ELECTRIC AG have announced 200 redundancies at their long-established factory in Winterthur, Switzerland. Production will continue at their main plant in Lausanne, according to the announcement.

Arcolite's Director General, Dr Franz Andres, told our reporter: "This represents a rationalization of our resources. We shall be creating 50 new jobs in our Lausanne plant. We have been wanting to expand on our Winterthur site for some time now, but this has finally proved to be uneconomic. I can assure our customers that there will be no interruption to supplies and we have sufficient stock to fill our current order book."

Arcolite shares fell from SF 3.220 to 2.975 on the Zurich Exchange after the announcement.

B To be on the safe side, Mr North wants you to find out about other suppliers. While he is away on a ten-day trip, you will be in charge. No local firms can supply the product, so you will have to contact possible suppliers abroad and ask for quotations.

Read this letter from Mr North to Jacques Roget, an old friend in the battery business. Decide what changes you would need to make if you were sending the letter to a business acquaintance, instead of an old friend like Jacques.

 BROADWAY AUTOS

444 Prince Rupert Avenue,
62008 Hentzau, Ruritania
TELEPHONE 77 1473 88999 (8 lines)
FAX +77 1473 889765

Jacques Roget
Rex et Cie
34 rue du Professeur Nicolas
35009 Clermont Ferrand
France

3 November 1998

Dear Jacques,

<u>Lightweight batteries</u>

I'm writing to you because we've been having a bit of trouble with one of our suppliers who makes the lightweight batteries we use to power our vehicles. I'm pretty sure you don't have a local distributor of your products in this country, which is why I'm writing to you direct to see if you can help us out. I did try to call, but you weren't available.

We require 4,800 units and delivery must be completed by 15 January 1999. A full specification of our requirements is given on the attached sheet, together with our technical brochure.

I'd appreciate it if you could quote us your best CIF price, giving a full specification of your product and shipping date. Of course our technical department would need to have some samples of the batteries to test in our laboratories before we could place a firm order.

We usually deal with new suppliers on the basis of payment in our currency by confirmed irrevocable letter of credit.

Assuming the lab tests go well, and you can quote us a competitive price, we'd certainly be able to place more substantial orders on a regular basis.

I'll be out of the office for a couple of weeks from tomorrow. In the meantime, do get in touch with one of my assistants if you need any more information.

Looking forward to hearing from you.

Give my regards to Jeanne and the kids.

Best,

Fred

Fred A. North, Buying Manager

Enclosed: specification and technical brochure

C *Work in pairs* Draft a short letter explaining your requirements, to be faxed to other battery companies. Your letter should be written in a more formal, impersonal style than Mr North's.

1 Introduce your firm and its products to the reader:

    We are ...

2 State the purpose of your letter:

    We are seeking a supplier of ...

3 Include a description or specification of the goods you require:

    A full specification of our requirements is given on the
    attached sheet.

4 Explain what you want the recipient to do:

    Please quote us your best price and shipping date.
    Before placing an order we would need to examine samples of the
    product.

5 State your terms and methods of payment:

    We usually pay by confirmed 60-day irrevocable letter of credit.

6 End on an optimistic note and request an early reply:

    There is a good prospect of our placing regular orders if ...
    We hope to be able to place further orders with you if ...
    We look forward to receiving an early reply.

➡ When you have written your first draft, show it to another pair. Look at their letter and consider these points:

- Does it cover all the essential points?   • Is it clear, concise and courteous?
- Does it sound natural and sincere?   • Will it create the right impression?
- Is it the kind of letter you'd like to receive yourself?

D [icon] Richard Duvall, your Production Manager, has suggested that you call his friend Jim Dale, the Sales Director of Dale & Sons Batteries in Manchester to ask him for a quotation.

Role-play the phone call:
Student A will play the role of Mr Dale. Look at File **13** for more information.
Student B will play the role of Mr North's assistant. Before you make the call, note down the questions that you want to ask Mr Dale.

Dale & Sons are proud to announce their NEW

Dale Hercules zinc cadmium power pack
the NEW lightweight battery for electric-powered vehicles

DALE BATTERIES: THE ORIGINAL AND STILL THE BEST

E The next day, in answer to one of your enquiries, you receive the fax on the next page. You've added your own notes in red ink. Read this information and then discuss the points below.

Artemis Batteries

33 Princess Flavia Square, Zenda
Telephone: 98 45 83   Telex 778303 TB   Fax 448908

1
Artemis can supply the product at 15% less than Arcolite.

3
Mr North may favour Rex because he knows Jacques Roget very well.

Mr Fred North
Purchasing Manager
Broadway Autos
Hentzau, Ruritania

2
Rex and Dale & Sons are both 10% lower than Arcolite.

9 November 1998

Dear Mr North,

Thank you very much for your enquiry. We are of course very familiar with your range of vehicles and are pleased to inform you that we have a new line in batteries that fit your specifications exactly.

The most suitable of our products for your requirements is the Artemis 66A Plus. This product combines economy with high power output. It is available now from stock.

I enclose a detailed quotation with prices, specifications and delivery terms. As you will see from this, our prices are very competitive.

I have instructed our agent Mr Martin of Fillmore S.A. to deliver five of these batteries to you next week, so that you can carry out the laboratory tests. Our own laboratory reports, enclosed with this letter, show that our new Artemis 66A Plus performs as well as any of our competitors' products and, in some respects, out-performs them.

If you would like further information, please telephone or fax me: my extension number is 776. Or you may prefer to contact Mr John Martin of Fillmore S.A. in Hentzau: his telephone number is 01 77 99 02.

I look forward to hearing from you,

Yours sincerely,

4
Latest reports say that Arcolite are in very good shape!

Decide what you should recommend to Mr North when he returns:

- Should you argue the case for having more than one supplier? Or should you have a sole supplier?
- If Arcolite agree to drop their price to the same level as Rex, should you then stick with Arcolite as sole supplier?
- Or should you favour Artemis? Or did your conversation with Mr Dale persuade you to favour Dale & Sons?

6.3 Answering enquiries

A **1** Imagine that you and your partner work in the export department of AntiSpy Products. It's your job to answer enquiries about your products. First, read this advertisement for your products:

Are you AFRAID . . . ?

... that someone has planted a bug somewhere in your office?

The battery-driven **AntiSpy™ CJ 4000 P** will detect any eavesdropping devices within 20 feet. It looks just like a Walkman and costs only $359.

... that people may overhear your confidential phone calls?

The **AntiSpy™ LR 44** "Octopus" portable telephone scrambler can be used anywhere in hotel rooms, phone booths, etc. Disguised in an ordinary executive briefcase, it costs only $299.

... that spies outside your building can "read" your computer screen? (Yes, it can and does happen – we ourselves sell equipment that can do this!)

Fit the NEW **AntiSpy™ SP 700** computer screen protector to each PC or workstation and you can stop worrying. The SP 700 fixes to any monitor and acts also as anti-reflection filter.

Special introductory price till May 1st while stocks last: $199 per unit or $499 for six. (Regular price $299)

All our prices are carriage paid by air.
Full no-argument money-back warranty on all our products.
Send $50 for catalog. Refundable against purchase.
All major credit cards accepted.

AntiSpy Products, 333 Rosedale Drive, Bakersfield, CA 93002, USA
Telephone: 555/453 9000   Telex: 87869
Fax: 9937

2 Now look at these notes. They give some ideas for a 'typical' answer to an enquiry by letter, fax or phone – or even to a personal enquiry.

Is there anything you'd add to these notes – or anything you wouldn't include?

1 Thank the customer for their interest in your product(s) and confirm that you can (or can't) help.

2 'Sell' your product and explain how it is suitable for your customer's needs.

3 Say that you're sending a catalogue, price list, advertising literature, etc.

4 Explain how the customer can get 'hands-on' experience of the product:
  • offer to send samples or get a rep to visit with samples/demo;
  • state the location of distributor's showroom near enquirer's address;
  • announce an exhibit at a forthcoming trade fair.

5 QUOTE:
- exactly what you are selling: confirm the specification of your product;
- prices in buyer's or another hard currency, including terms of delivery (CIF, DDP, FOB, etc.) and validity:

      Total: 3,450 US dollars CIF.
      The prices shown in this offer are valid for a period
      of 60 days from the date hereof.

- discounts: for cash/bulk, etc.;
- terms of payment: cash with order / open account / letter of credit, etc.*:

      Payment by irrevocable letter of credit in US dollars
      on a United States bank, allowing part-shipment, trans-
      shipment and house bills, and valid for 90 days from
      order date.
      Payment with order by banker's draft or cheque on a US
      bank.

- shipping date:

      The goods will be ready for shipment 3 to 4 weeks from
      receipt of your written order and confirmation of your
      letter of credit.

6 End on an optimistic note and encourage the customer to phone or fax you personally for more information.

* Terms of payment are covered in more detail in Unit 7.

3 Here is a printout of your current stock position and prices. You'll need to refer to this again during the activity.

AntiSpy Products Inc.

Inventory position and prices	April 7, 1999

CJ 4000P BUG DETECTOR
Stock now: 45
Next delivery to warehouse: Jun 15   Quantity: 100
List price: $359 CIF   Discounts: 5+ 20%   10+ 25%

LR 44 "OCTOPUS" TELEPHONE SCRAMBLER
Stock now: 9
Next delivery to warehouse: Aug 15   Quantity: 300
List price: $299 CIF   Discounts: 5+ 20%   10+ 25%
Note: Customer must acquire import license for this product (CCCN 0303 8100)

SP 700 SCREEN PROTECTOR
Stock now: 75
Next delivery to warehouse: May 30   Quantity: 500
List price: $299 CIF
Offer price to May 1st: $199 $499 for six
Notes: Customer must specify size and make of screens to be fitted
Normal discounts do not apply before May 1st

GR 440 SCREEN SPY
List price: $2950 FOB airport
Available to special order only, cash with order. Customer must provide import license
(CCCN 4102 2000). Ready for shipment date: 12 months from date of order

B *Work in pairs* Using the information given in the advertisement and the printout in **A**, draft replies to Enquiries **#1** and **#2**.

➡ After you have written each draft, show it to another pair and discuss these questions:

- Does it cover all the essential points?
- Is it clear, concise and courteous?
- Will it create the right impression?
- Is it the kind of letter or fax you would like to receive yourself?

- Is the information correct?
- Does it sound natural and sincere?

Enquiry #1

Please send your catalog and charge my American Express Card
#667589980 — Expiration date August 15, 1999.

Regards Hanson,
Johnson Oil, Brisbane, Australia

Thank you   sending you our catalogue
Debited your American Express card $50 US
$50 will be discounted from your purchase
Get in touch with me if you have any queries

Enquiry #2

Do you supply a portable listening device detector? *Yes* Is this available
from stock? Please quote your best DDP air freight price for five.

Sincerely, *Yes*

José Perez, Andes Mining Co, Bogotá, Colombia

Quote price – all our prices include shipping

$50 secures our complete 120 pp catalogue

C 🔘🔘 *Work in pairs* You'll hear a phone call: one of your colleagues is on the phone to Japan. Listen to what he says and alter the inventory position on your printout in **A ③**.
Then draft replies to Enquiries **#3** and **#4**. Again, get another pair to evaluate each of your drafts.

Enquiry #3

I would like to know about the availability of a telephone
scrambler. If you have one, please let me know the price. Is
this product suitable for both tone dial and pulse dial? Also
is it suitable for different voltages?

Best, Mary Graham

Quote prices   Available now / from Aug 15
Yes to both suitability queries
Catalogue $50

Enquiry #4

Mr Ovambo from Lagos, Nigeria wants
to know about the Screen Protector.
He needs 10 for customers of his.

Sorry we can't supply - import restrictions
into Nigeria introduced last year.
Our former distributor (Kano Security,
Independence Square, Kano) may still
have stocks.

D 🔲 *Work in pairs* Now you will have to deal with two more enquiries on the phone.

One of you should look at File **14**, the other at **42**.

The first enquiry concerns this fax:

> We require urgent information on behalf of a customer about your telephone scrambler:
> Is the battery pack rechargeable on 110 volt current?
> Is it true that its operation can interfere with other phones in the same building?
>
> Please phone us after 12 noon your time.
>
> Regards, J. Gomez, Agencia Léon, Mexico City

E *Work in groups or as a class* Discuss these questions:
- Which of the enquiries was most difficult to deal with? Why was this?
- What can go wrong when dealing with enquiries? How can such problems be avoided?
- How are the enquiries you've dealt with in your present job (or a previous job) different from the ones you had to do in this activity?

6.4 Placing and filling orders

Your role

Work in pairs You and your partner work in the Export Department of Sunworld Powerboats. Mr Richardson, your boss, has found a promising new customer in Central America. Because of the time difference, and the difficulty of getting through by phone, you can only communicate with this customer by fax or letter ...

A **Today is Friday, 12 July**

Look at this quotation, which you are about to fax to the customer.
Check it through to make sure there are no mistakes. Make any necessary alterations before you send it.

FAX

FROM **SUNWORLD POWERBOATS**
+44 1202 777990

TO   Naves Limón, Puerto Limón, Costa Rica
+506 778855

Our Quotation No: 0067 12 July 1999   15.33

Thank you for your enquiry about our PB 5000 30-foot SunVoyager.
You asked us to give you our best CIF price for two of these.

The price for two PB 5000 with specifications as in our 1999
catalogue pages 42–45 is 179,800 (one seven eight thousand nine
hundred) United States Dollars CIF Puerto Limón.

If you require the special stainless steel anchors and chains
(our catalogue numbers: 5567 and 8876), the total price is
187,850 US Dollars.

The goods will be ready for shipment 3 to 4 weeks from the date
of your written order. We pack each PB 5000 for expert in a 40-
foot open top container. We understand from our freight
forwarders that Cariblines have a scheduled service to Puerto
Limón once a month.

We would appreciate payment by irrevocable Letter of Credit
confirmed on a London bank and valid for 90 (nine) days from the
date of your order. The prices given in this offer are valid for
a period of thirty days from the date of this fax.

We look forward to hearing from you.

If you require further information, I shall be pleased to help
you personally.

Mr Richards sends his best regards.

Best wishes,

SUNWORLD POWERBOATS

B **Today is Thursday, 18 July**

Look at File **16**, where you will see the order from Costa Rica. Check it against your quotation above.

Before you can give a firm shipping date, you will need to get a delivery date from Alpha Marine, your supplier of anchors. Send them a fax to order two anchors from their catalogue:

3456	Anchor, stainless steel, 120 kg	£135 including delivery

C Today is Friday, 19 July

Your production manager promises both vessels packed for export in containers on 22 August – if the special anchors are available.

Look at File **46** to see two faxes: one from Alpha Marine and the other from your freight forwarders.

1 Fax an acknowledgement of the order to Naves Limón:
- Confirm the terms of payment and delivery.
- Quote a firm shipping date.
- Say that you're sending a proforma invoice by airmail today.

2 Draft a short letter to accompany the proforma invoice.

D Today is Friday, 13 September

Two months have passed, you have shipped the goods and by now they should have arrived. Unfortunately, there's a worrying headline in today's paper:

Hurricane Suzy hits Caribbean

Look at File **71** to see a fax from Costa Rica. Reply to the fax and take any other action you think necessary.

E Today is Friday, 15 November

Look at File **22** to see a memo from Mr Richardson and take appropriate action.

F Today is Friday, 20 December

Fax a short Christmas message to Naves Limón.

G Today is Monday, 23 December

Look at File **52** and take appropriate action.

H *Work in groups* Discuss these questions:
- How do the idealized events in the Sunworld scenario relate to your own real-life experiences of making and answering enquiries?
- What other procedures need to be carried out, which were assumed to have been done in the Sunworld scenario?
- Think of all the tasks you performed in this activity – which were the most difficult? Why?

7 Money matters

7.1 Dealing with figures

A *Work in pairs* Look at the pictures and discuss
these questions:

- What are the people in the photos doing?
- When was the last time you dealt with figures
  or numbers in English? What did you do?
- How much of your time do you spend dealing
  with figures?

B *Work in pairs* Here are some phrases using numbers in payments. Decide which of the phrases on the right go with which figures on the left.

1	Invoice No. 508/19G
2	a gross profit of 14.5 %
3	31 August 1997
4	The list price is £41,337
5	profit before interest and tax of £1,457,000
6	an annual rate of interest of 26.8 %
7	a handling charge of 1½ %
8	total interest charges of £3.66
9	$673m operating profits

a	three pounds sixty-six
b	fourteen point five per cent
c	twenty-six point eight per cent
d	forty-one thousand three hundred and thirty-seven
e	one million four hundred and fifty-seven thousand
f	seventeen hundred and ninety-five
g	six hundred and seventy-three million
h	the thirty-first of August nineteen ninety-seven
i	three point six six
j	one and a half per cent
k	five o eight stroke nineteen G *or* five zero eight oblique nineteen G
l	one and a quarter per cent

➡ Which items are left over? Write them out as figures.

C **1** ◎◎ Listen to the recording and complete the information missing from this report of a company's financial performance.

LVMH advances in slowing market

LVMH, the French luxury goods group which owns a string of prestige brand names ranging from Louis Vuitton luggage to Hennessy cognac, saw net profits rise by _____ to FFr 1.29bn ($ _____) from FFr _____ in the first half of the year in spite of the downturn in the luxury products industry.

The group saw overall group sales in the first six months of this year rise by _____ to FFr _____ from 9.26bn in the same period last year.

Operating income showed a marginal increase to FFr _____ from 2.34bn.

Wines and spirits, which have borne the brunt of the economic slowdown, suffered a fall in sales to FFr 4.44bn from FFr _____ , while operating profits slipped to FFr 1.26bn from 1.51bn.

Luggage and leather products were also affected by Japan's instability, but managed to increase operating profits to FFr _____ from 827m on sales up to FFr 2.33bn from 2.15bn.

Perfumes and cosmetics benefited from the launch of Dune, a new Christian Dior fragrance, and Amarige, under the Givenchy umbrella.

Sales rose to FFr 2.54bn from _____ and operating profits to FFr 330m from _____

LVMH earlier this week relaunched Miss Dior, one of its classic scents.

② *Work in pairs* Use the information you now have to work out the following amounts:

a) the rise in net profits in the first half of the year
b) the difference in overall group sales in the first six months
c) the fall in sales for wines and spirits
d) the increase in operating profits for luggage and leather products
e) the difference in sales of perfumes and cosmetics

D [≈≈≈] *Work in pairs* One of you should look at File **17**, the other at **47**. You'll each have an air waybill, the document that accompanies air freight, with incomplete figures to fill in.

Phone your partner to find out what the missing details are.

Ask your partner to dictate them to you. Your partner will also require details from you.

7.2 Cash flow

① *Work in pairs* Read this article containing advice on dealing with cash-flow problems. Decide what sort of people the article is written for. Which pieces of advice do you find most helpful?

Late payers can kill a business

MANAGING CASH FLOW in the everyday sense is about making sure you have money coming in to finance the costs of the goods and services you are producing.

If you're a small business, the chances are that for every £100 you owe, others owe you £155. What's more, you're probably waiting up to 12 weeks to get paid. It's not right. Some business people have very definite ideas about what should be done to make things fairer.

Improving credit control can make a world of difference to your business prospects. Profit is good, but it's cash that pays the wages.

So here are ten tips to help you get what's due to you.

1 ASSESS the credit risk of every customer and assign a credit limit to them before any goods are supplied. Trade and bank references should always be taken up before accepting a customer on credit terms.

2 STATE the credit terms clearly on each invoice (a pay-by date and details of interest charges).

3 ASK for a percentage of the invoice value in advance as protection against bad debt and to help cash flow.

4 TRY credit insurance if credit checks do not come up to standard. It's not always available, but it can provide up to 100 per cent cover on approved debts, guaranteeing payment by a specified date.

5 THINK about using debt collection agencies for smaller debts. Agency fees, usually based on a percentage, are only payable if the debt is successfully recovered.

6 INVESTIGATE the potential of factoring. Factors purchase a firm's unpaid invoices, paying up to 70 per cent or more of the face value, but they often only take on the best customers.

7 MAKE SURE you know the name and department of the person to whom each invoice is being sent.

8 CHECK how long existing customers take to pay – and negotiate new credit terms if they're not meeting bills on time.

9 OFFER your customers discounts for paying up promptly when invoiced.

10 FOLLOW UP with a fax to make sure your invoice isn't overlooked, disregarded or left at the bottom of the pile.

2 Read the article once more and match up these statements with the points in the article.

According to the article ...

a) How can you deal with smaller debts?
b) What is a good way of protecting yourself against bad debts?
c) What should you do if present customers delay in paying?
d) What should you do in order to be sure your invoice has not been forgotten?
e) What should you do before sending goods to a customer?
f) When should you use credit insurance?
g) What can you do if customers pay up swiftly?
h) How do factors work?
i) What should you write clearly on the invoice?
j) Whose name do you need to know?

3 Discuss these questions:

- Which of the above methods are you familiar with in your own country and company (or a company you have worked for)?
- How useful is such advice in your country?

7.3 Changing prices: Dealing with invoicing errors

A *Work in pairs* Imagine that you and your partner have been working in the Accounts Department of Finntec for two weeks. Your boss Ms Aaltio has asked you to fill in the invoice for Frigorifico Ameglio S.A. Use these documents to bill and invoice the client.

FINNTEC

P. O. Box 325
SF–33200 Tampere

PRICE LIST 1999

Item: Sensor Switches			
Type	Price	Type	Price
A3A	$1.50	A6D	$1.80
A3B	$0.80	A6T	$1.30
B3F	$1.70	A7G	$0.90
B3J	$2.20	A7H	$1.35
10% discount on bulk orders 20 gross plus			

FINNTEC
P.O. Box 325
SF - 33200 TAMPERE
FINLAND

© SITPRO
1992

INVOICE RECHNUNG FACTURE FACTURA فاتـــورة

Invoice number
04276

Invoice date (tax point)	Seller's reference
1 February 1999	LS 43351/91

Buyer's reference	Other reference

U N I C

Consignee	VAT no.	Buyer (if not consignee)	VAT no.
N/A			

Country of origin of goods	Country of destination

Terms of delivery and payment

Payment against accompanied by documents through Rabobank

Vessel/flight no. and date	Port/airport of loading
MS JUPITER	HELSINKI

Port/airport of discharge	Place of delivery
MONTEVIDEO	

Shipping marks: container number	No. and kind of packages: description of goods	Commodity code	Total gross wt (Kg)	Total cube (m3)
UU LS 433				
			Total net wt(Kg)	

Item/packages	Gross/net/cube	Description	Quantity	Unit price	Amount
1					
				Invoice total	

Finntec
P.O. Box 325
SF—33200 Tampere
Finland
Telefax: +358 31 134 845
Your Ref: Customer No.: 645
For the Attn of G. Aaltio   20 January 1999

Thanks for your quotation 9302.
We wish to order 35 gross of Type A6D Switches.

Please deliver asap.

Sincerely,

Julio Martinez

Julio Martinez

Customer No.: 645
Order: 03764   **Quantity items:** 35 gross
Address: Frigorifico Ameglio S.A., Colonia 1023, Montevideo, Uruguay
Description of merchandise: sensor switches type A6D

Method of payment: Irrevocable Letter of Credit with documents
Terms of payment agreed: draft sight
Method of payment agreed: FOB Helsinki
Payment due: on presentation

B ⟨☜⟩ You've just found out that new prices have been in operation for two weeks, so you need to contact the customer. One of you looks at File **18** and phones the customer, the other looks at File **48** and plays the role of Julio Martinez.

7.3 Changing prices: Dealing with invoicing errors

C Three days later you receive a letter from Julio Martinez. Look at File **85** to see this and then draft an answer to the letter.

D A few weeks later you receive a fax from Julio Martinez (you can see it in File **72**). Draft the acknowledgement which Mr Martinez of Frigorifico Ameglio S.A. has requested. Include this phrase: We thank you for your remittance of ...

7.4 Letters of Credit

Irrevocable Letter of Credit

BARCLAYS BANK PLC
MANCHESTER INTERNATIONAL SERVICES BRANCH
THIRD FLOOR, 51 MOSLEY STREET, MANCHESTER M60 2BU. UK.
PHONE: 061 228 3322 TELEX: 667565 ANSWERBK: BARMAN G

BENEFICIARY:
NATHAN AND COLES LIMITED
1 NATHAN ROAD
LONDON SE11 8JB
UNITED KINGDOM

2

ADVICE OF
IRREVOCABLE DOCUMENTARY CREDIT **5**
NUMBER: TODC 603921
DATED 20TH JUNE 1994
DATE OF EXPIRY: 31ST AUGUST 1994
PLACE OF EXPIRY: UNITED KINGDOM
AMOUNT: UP TO GBP 160,000.00 **6**
UP TO ONE HUNDRED SIXTY THOUSAND
AND 00/100'S POUNDS STERLING
OUR ADVICE NUMBER: MRDC708447

OPENING BANK:
BARCLAYS BANK OF CANADA
PO BOX 377
COMMERCE COURT POSTAL STATION
TORONTO, ONTARIO
CANADA

APPLICANT:
MURRAY CORPORATION LIMITED **7**
1052 CAUSEWAY BOULEVARD
TORONTO

30TH JUNE 1994

DEAR SIR(S)

THIS LETTER OF CREDIT IS AVAILABLE WITH BARCLAYS BANK PLC: BY PAYMENT AGAINST PRESENTATION OF THE DOCUMENTS **8**
DETAILED HEREIN AND OF YOUR DRAFTS AT SIGHT DRAWN ON BARCLAYS BANK PLC, MANCHESTER FOR 100 PER CENT OF
INVOICE VALUE.

3 DOCUMENTS REQUIRED:-

1 - COMMERCIAL INVOICE IN QUADRUPLICATE
2 - INSURANCE POLICY/CERTIFICATE IN DUPLICATE COVERING MARINE AND WAR RISKS FOR 110 PER CENT OF THE INVOICE
    VALUE
3 - FULL SET OF CLEAN ON BOARD BLANK ENDORSED PORT TO PORT BILLS OF LADING MARKED NOTIFY MURRAY
    CORPORATION LIMITED, 1052 CAUSEWAY BOULEVARD, TORONTO, ONTARIO.

COVERING THE FOLLOWING GOODS:-

16 - PRINTING MACHINES NATHAN AND COLES MODEL CAXTON EXCELSIOR 1470 **9**
4 — COST, INSURANCE & FREIGHT TORONTO
     PARTIAL SHIPMENTS: NOT ALLOWED
     TRANSHIPMENTS: ALLOWED **10**
     SHIPMENT FROM: UK PORT
     NO LATER THAN: 15TH AUGUST 1994 **11**
     FOR TRANSPORTATION TO: TORONTO

DOCUMENTS MUST BE PRESENTED AT PLACE OF EXPIRATION WITHIN 15 DAYS OF ISSUE DATE OF TRANSPORT DOCUMENT AND
WITHIN THE L/C VALIDITY.

DOCUMENTS ARE TO BE ACCOMPANIED BY YOUR DRAFTS DRAWN ON BARCLAYS BANK PLC AT SIGHT MARKED 'DRAWN UNDER
IRREVOCABLE LETTER OF CREDIT NO TODC 603921 OF BARCLAYS BANK OF CANADA AND QUOTING OUR REFERENCE NUMBER
MRDC708447.

IMPORTANT: PLEASE CAREFULLY CHECK THE DETAILS OF THIS CREDIT AS IT IS ESSENTIAL THAT DOCUMENTS TENDERED
CONFORM IN EVERY RESPECT WITH THE CREDIT TERMS. IF YOU ARE UNABLE TO COMPLY, PLEASE COMMUNICATE WITH YOUR
BUYERS PROMPTLY IN ORDER THAT THEY MAY ARRANGE A SUITABLE AMENDMENT WITHOUT DELAY. IF DOCUMENTS ARE
PRESENTED WHICH DIFFER FROM THE CREDIT TERMS, WE RESERVE THE RIGHT TO MAKE AN ADDITIONAL CHARGE.

WE ADD OUR CONFIRMATION TO THIS CREDIT AND UNDERTAKE THAT DRAFT(S) AND DOCUMENTS DRAWN UNDER AND IN
STRICT CONFORMITY WITH THE TERMS THEREOF WILL BE HONOURED ON PRESENTATION.

THIS CREDIT IS SUBJECT TO THE UNIFORM CUSTOMS AND PRACTICE FOR DOCUMENTARY CREDITS (1993 REVISION), ICC
PUBLICATION NUMBER 500.

YOURS FAITHFULLY

SPECIMEN   SPECIMEN

....
AUTHORISED SIGNATURE   AUTHORISED SIGNATURE

A *Work in pairs* Look at the document opposite. Read the explanations below of the various sections, and agree which explanation goes with which number in the document.

The Documentary Letter of Credit is a form of payment widely used in foreign trade. Most credits are similar in appearance and contain the following details:

The terms of contract and shipment (i.e. whether 'EXW', 'FOB', 'CIF', etc.)

The name and address of the importer

Whether the credit is available for one or several partshipments

The amount of the credit, in sterling or a foreign currency

The expiry date

A brief description of the goods covered by the credit

The name and address of the exporter

Precise instructions as to the documents against which payment is to be made

The type of credit (revocable or irrevocable)

Shipping details, including whether partshipments and/or transhipments are allowed. Also recorded should be the latest date for shipment and the names of the ports of shipment and discharge. (It may be in the best interest of the exporter for shipment to be allowed 'from any UK port' so that a choice is available if, for example, some ports are affected by strikes. The same applies for the port of discharge.)

The name of the party on whom the bills of exchange are to be drawn, and whether they are to be at sight or of a particular tenor

➡ See File **73** for the correct numbered order.

B ◎◎ You'll hear a recording of a banker talking about some of the common mistakes that are made when people complete letters of credit. Fill in the items missing below:

Results of the survey:

Reasons for rejecting 25% of the documents:

- the letter of credit had 1 _____
- the documents were presented 2 _____ the period stipulated in the letter of credit
- the shipment was 3 _____

Documents were often inconsistent with one another in the following ways:

- the description (or 4 _____) of goods on invoice(s) differed from that in the letter of credit
- the 5 _____ differed between export documents
- the amounts of 6 _____ shown on the invoice(s) and bill of exchange (draft) differed
- the 7 _____ differed between documents
- the letter of credit was 8 _____ the value of the order
- the 9 _____ was short
- some documents 10 _____
- 11 _____ , where required, on documents presented
- 12 _____ were used when not allowed

C *Work in groups* Compare your answers. Then discuss these questions:
- What are your own personal experiences with documents involving figures?
- What advice can you give each other on how to deal with forms and complex documentation?

7.5 Chasing payment

A ◎◎ *Work in pairs* You'll hear a telephone conversation between a credit controller, Valentina Santinelli, and a customer, Wilhelm Becker, who hasn't paid an outstanding bill.

1 Listen and mark whether the statements below are true ☑ or false ☒:

The credit controller …

1	has no sympathy with the customer	☒
2	offers a bank overdraft	☒
3	threatens legal action	☐
4	grants an extra week's credit	☐
5	insists on prompt payment	☐
6	suggests there may be a change in conditions of payment	☐

2 Listen a second time and complete the notes with the reasons (or excuses) that the customer gives for the late payment.

> *1st reason:*   *(request for an extension of credit)*
> *2nd reason: company*
> *Another reason: our*   *have to be considered*
> *Major problem:*   *– number*
> *of outstanding accounts ourselves*
> *Our bank*   *us to overdraw our account*
> *We have given a major client who owes us a lot of money*
>
> *Another customer who owes us a lot of money*

B Imagine you are assisting the credit controller, Valentina Santinelli. Draft a letter for her to read. It is the end of the month and you still have not received any payment on the invoice from Wilhelm Becker. Write a first reminder to them. You aren't satisfied with your customer's delay. But you still want to give them a chance to pay up …

Complete this first reminder letter:

```
Dear Mr Becker,

According to our records, payment of our invoice, no. 35823,
```

- explain that you have received no payment
- quote your terms of business: 30 days net
- mention the delay of 90 days

- state your company's policy on unsettled debts
- express your unwillingness to take court action
- request payment immediately
- state that you enclose a copy of the invoice

Yours sincerely,

Valentina Santinelli

(Credit Controller)

C A week later you receive this letter:

3 August 1999

Dear Ms Santinelli,

As you will remember from our telephone call, we have recently been experiencing a number of difficulties with several large customers. This has resulted in unfortunate delays in paying outstanding accounts.

We are extremely sorry that your company has been affected by these developments.

We are doing everything possible to rectify the situation. Indeed we hope to be able to settle our debts within the very near future.

I would very much appreciate it if you could bear with us patiently, as I am sure that liquidation on our part would not be in your interest either.

Yours sincerely,

Wilhelm Becker

(Chief clerk, Accounts)

Decide what to do. Will you write a second reminder or phone them up?

Draft a letter or fax OR make a further phone call to find out what the problem is.

🗣 If you decide to make a phone call, student A plays the role of the credit controller and looks at File **19** and makes the phone call. Student B looks at File **27**, playing the customer.

D You receive a letter with a cheque. Look at File **74** and decide how to react.

8 Dealing with problems

8.1 What seems to be the problem?

A *Work in pairs* Look at these pictures:
- What do you think has happened?
- What are the people going to say?
- What would you do in each situation?

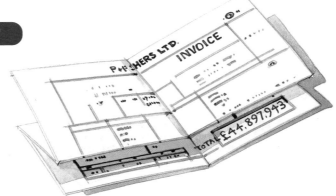

B 🎧 You'll hear eight short phone calls. Match the NUMBER of each call to one of these sentences. Put a ring round the number of the call on the right. The first two are done as examples.

Be careful: one sentence in each group is a 'wrong answer'!

a The customer was sent only one set instead of three.   ① 2
b The customer wants to be sent one set of three items.   1 2
c The customer was sent three sets instead of one.   1 ②

d The speaker will arrive late because of the heavy traffic on the way
   to the airport and now expects to arrive at 1.45.   3 4
e The speaker will arrive late because of delays at the airport and now
   expects to arrive at 4.45.   3 4
f The speaker will arrive late because of the heavy traffic and now
   expects to arrive at 1.45.   3 4

g The customer wants the damaged goods to be replaced.   5 6

h The customer wants his/her account to be credited for the damaged
   goods.   5 6

i The customer refuses to pay for the damaged goods.   5 6

j The faulty machine has to be replaced.   7 8

k The faulty machine has not been repaired satisfactorily.   7 8

l The faulty machine needs to be repaired.   7 8

C *Work in groups* Discuss these questions with your partners:

- What problems have you had in your work or work experience that led to complaints or apologies?
- What is the worst mistake you've made in your work or work experience? What happened? How could you have avoided it?
- What kind of problems might people expect in these departments of a company:

  accounts   personnel   sales   warehouse   factory   transport   purchasing

8.2 We all make mistakes – sometimes!

A *Work in pairs or small groups* You work in the buying department at Zenith International. You have just got back from holiday. While you were away Max, the 19-year-old son of your director, was in charge of your office …

This is a note you left for Max before you went away:

> Max, while I'm away please place an order for 45
> x 100 metre reels of 40mm MCL88 cable from
> Uniflex SpA in La Spezia, Italy. All the details
> are in the files.
> This is a repeat order — just copy the previous
> one and change the dates.

and this is a note that Max has left for you:

> MCL 88 cable ordered as you instructed.
> You'll be pleased to know that the
> price has gone down since your last
> order! And Uniplex seem to have
> moved from La Spezia to Pisa.
> Their new address is:
> Uniplex srl, Viale Dell'Industria 131,
> 56100 Pisa
> Best wishes,
> Max
> P.S. Hope you had a good holiday!

➡ What do you think may have happened? What should you do?

B ◎◎ Listen to a telephone message that was recorded on your answering machine yesterday.

Then look at File **75** to see two more documents, including a fax that has just arrived.

Decide what you are going to do:

- Will you stick by Max's order, which will upset the people you know at UNIFLEX SpA?
- Uniplex's price is 7½% lower than UNIFLEX's.
  Will you try to negotiate a lower price from UNIFLEX? Or is it better to explain to Uniplex what has happened, apologize and cancel the order?
- Will you phone or write to both firms? Or will you make a personal visit to them while you're in Italy next week?

C 🗣️ or 👥 When you've decided what to do in **B**, role-play the two phone calls or visits: one to Piero Conti at Uniplex srl and the other to Lucia Donato at UNIFLEX SpA. Tell them what you have decided.

➡ **Plan each call or visit, by making notes before you begin.**
(One of you will have to play the role of the Italian supplier in each role-play.)

> *I'm afraid there's been a bit of a misunderstanding. You see ...*
> *I'm not quite sure how to put this, but ...*
> *There's been a slight mix-up about one of our orders ...*

D Draft a fax to Uniplex and another to UNIFLEX, which you could have sent *instead of* phoning or visiting them.

Send your faxes to another group and ask for their reactions and comments.

E Explain to the rest of the class (or another group) how you dealt with the problems.

F Draft a short report explaining how you dealt with the problems, for the attention of your boss. Don't forget that he is Max's father!

"Cost savings are one thing, Harris, but we'd never get away with Velcro door latches."

8.3 Complaining and apologizing

Preparation

at ** Read this information and highlight the phrases and expressions you find useful. Try to use them in the practice that follows in steps **B**, **C** and **D**.

If you want to complain to a person you don't know well, be careful! A direct complaint or criticism can sound very rude or aggressive.

It may be best to mention the problem more indirectly by saying:

> *I'm sorry to have to say this but ...*
> *I'm sorry to bother you but ...*
> *I think you may have forgotten ...*
> *It may have slipped your mind, but ...*
> *There may have been a misunderstanding about ...*

In some situations, but only if you're talking to someone you know really well, it may be necessary to say more directly:

> *What are you going to do about ...?*
> *I'm not at all satisfied with ...*

But only in extreme cases, if you've already tried more polite methods, would you have to threaten someone:

> *Look, if you don't send your engineer to repair the machine, we will be forced/obliged to cancel our next order.*

> `Unless you pay the account within seven days,`
> `we will place the matter in the hands of our`
> `solicitors/attorneys ...`

If someone complains to you, or if you think they're likely to complain, it may be wise to apologize – even if it wasn't really your fault. Then you can promise to put things right:

> *Sorry, my fault.*
> *I'm very sorry. I didn't realize.*
> *There has been a slip-up/problem in our ... dept.*

> `We are very sorry about the delay/mistake ...`
> `We wish to apologize for ...`
> `Please accept our apologies for ...`

You can accept someone's apology by saying:

> *That's all right!*
> *It's perfectly all right.*
> *It really doesn't matter.*

A 🔘🔘 You'll hear four conversations. Note down what the PROBLEM is in each case and what ACTION is to be taken.

PROBLEM   ACTION to be taken
1 Wrong size .... — wrongly .... box   refund: £ ....
2
3   AND
4

B *Work in pairs* Look at these extracts from four letters. Complete each sentence. Then decide what to write in your reply to each as if it was *your fault* in each case.

we are concerned that the order we placed by letter on 8 June may have got lost in the post. Could you please

the order has not yet arrived at our warehouse, even though we received advice of shipping from you ten days ago. Would you

according to your scale of charges the price of a single room with bath is $55 including tax. However, on checking my account later I discovered that I was charged $69.50 per night. Will you please

our order was for 80 boxes containing 144 items each. Each box we have opened so far contains only 100 items. Will you please

C 🔲🔲🔲 *Work in pairs* Now imagine that the four problems in **B** are being discussed on the phone. Role-play each conversation with your partner. Take it in turns to be the customer.

D *Work in small groups* Look at this information and decide what other excuses you can add to the list below.

> If things have gone wrong, the person you're talking to will want to know the *reasons*. He or she may assume that someone (or everyone) in your firm is to blame and that they've been:
>
> inefficient   clumsy   slow   careless   impolite   forgetful *or* unhelpful
>
> If you don't want to accept responsibility or blame another person, you could offer an excuse. For example:
>
> a clerical error   a computer error   a shortage of staff

E *Work in pairs* One of you should look at File **20**, the other at **51**. This time you will be dealing with some problems that might arise when working with an English-speaking colleague.

Here are some useful expressions you can use to introduce a criticism:

> *I'm sorry to mention this, but ...   I'm not quite sure how to put this, but ...*
> *There's something I've been meaning to tell you: ...*

8.4 Friday afternoon: Delivery problems

Work in pairs or in small groups Discuss what action you would take in these situations. In each case, imagine that it's Friday afternoon …

A You work in the PURCHASING DEPARTMENT of Pacific International, a manufacturer. Last month you placed an order with Ocean View Supplies Inc. of New Jersey for some special components. The goods were delivered on Monday. Now it's 3pm on Friday.

1 ◎◎ Your production manager, Mr Robinson, has left a message for you on the telephone answering machine. Make notes as you listen to the recording.

2 In 1995, in connection with a different order, you sent Ocean View this fax. Read it through. When was delivery promised for?

FAX #0097   05/06/95
_____

FROM Pacific International **TO** Fred Duvall, Ocean View Supplies

Re: Our order TR 678

Last month we ordered from you 120 boxes of your article No. 231. You promised delivery on 30 May 1995. So far we have not received this shipment and have not heard from you.

Please arrange for immediate shipment and inform us when the shipment will arrive here.

Regards,

Pat Brown

---

③ Now read this reply which you received from Ocean View shortly afterwards. What reason was given for the delay?

Ocean View Supplies Inc.

1459 Atlantic Drive, Asbury Park, NJ 07712

Pat Brown
Purchasing Manager
Pacific International

7/6/95

Re: Your fax #0097 dated 05-06-95

Dear Mr Brown,

Thank you for your fax. We are very sorry for the delay in shipping your order.

We normally pride ourselves on keeping to our delivery dates, but in this case our suppliers shipped to us late and the components did not arrive here till last Wednesday. I am glad to be able to say that your order is being packed for export now.

We will ship the goods on June 9 ex Newark to Rotterdam. The shipment will arrive in London on June 17.

Again, we are very sorry, but it was beyond our control. We greatly regret any inconvenience that may have been caused.

Best,

Fred Duvall

Ocean View Supplies

---

④ Decide what you are going to do:
- What will you tell Mr Robinson?
- Will you telephone Ocean View, fax them or send them a letter?
- What will you say or write?

⑤ Draft a letter or fax – or make notes for a phone call.

B You are responsible for Export CUSTOMER SERVICE at Atlantic International.

① Read this memo from Mr Frost, your delivery manager:

We have just had Arctic Refrigeration on the phone about the order we sent out last week. They say that the goods were damaged when they inspected them, but they didn't notice this till two days after delivery. My driver got their signature to confirm that the shipment was in good condition on delivery. My guess is that Arctic's people caused the damage and they are trying to blame us. They are claiming credit of $535 on their next order.
Please sort this one out before the end of today, Friday.

And read this fax from your customers, Arctic Refrigeration:

Your delivery manager was most unhelpful on the telephone. He implied that we are responsible for the damage caused by your driver! My warehouse manager informs me that this man unloaded the shipment without sufficient care for the fragile nature of the contents of the cartons.

We expect to receive $585 credit on our next order. A detailed list of the damage is on page 2 of this fax.

Please reply to this fax by return.

② Decide together what you are going to do. How will you solve this problem? What will you tell Mr Frost? What will you say or write to Arctic Refrigeration?

③ Draft a letter or fax to Arctic Refrigeration – or make notes for the phone call you will make.

C *Work in groups or as a whole class* Discuss these questions:
- How do you prefer to deal with problems: face-to-face, by phone or in writing? Why?
- Is it best to take the blame, or to blame someone else for your mistake?
- Is it always best to tell the truth when someone is at fault? Why/Why not?

8.5 Only the best is good enough ...

A *Work in pairs* Look at these opinions. Which do you agree with ☑ and which do you disagree with ☒?

☐ *"Customers will pay top prices for a high quality product."*
☐ *"Customers generally prefer a low cost product."*
☐ *"Nobody's perfect – we all make mistakes sometimes."*
☐ *"In every firm there are some people who aren't interested in improving the quality of the products."*
☐ *"You can't rely on workers to produce high quality goods unless someone supervises their work all the time."*
☐ *"A company can't influence its suppliers' manufacturing methods."*
☐ *"It's easy for big companies to force small suppliers to obey their rules."*

B **①** ◎◎ You'll hear an interview with a management consultant. Each sentence in this summary contains ONE mistake. Underline each of the mistakes and correct them.

1 Quality affects every function of the company and <u>some</u> of its employees. ..*all*...
2 With 'Zero Defects' the company aims to produce goods that are mostly perfect. ....
3 In the past, customers expected some faults – they could be corrected by apologizing to the supplier, who would replace the faulty goods. ....
4 Putting mistakes right is labour-intensive and inexpensive and it's more cost-effective to produce a perfect product with no defects. ....
5 If your competitors can produce perfect products, your customers will prefer yours. ....
6 A service has to be so good that there is no dissatisfaction and there are few complaints from your clients. ....
7 A manufacturer can change suppliers to get materials of the highest quality, even if this means paying less. ....
8 The extra cost is justified if the quality of your own production deteriorates. ....
9 To introduce Quality you must sell the idea to everyone in the company: most of the staff have to believe in quality. ....
10 It's easier to sell new ideas to established staff. ....

2 *Work in groups* Discuss these questions:
- How does the concept of Total Quality relate to the products or services of your company (or a company you know)?
- How can Total Quality be applied to non-commercial services, such as education, public health and public transport?

C **1** *Work in groups* Look at these documents and then discuss the questions below:

Our Mission: Delight our Customers

Something typically happens as a company grows—
it loses touch with delighting the customer.
Not in this case . . .
CE Software is committed to continuing to delight you
by improving your computing and global environments.
Whether it's our use of environmentally friendly packaging
or our award-winning user interfaces, we are committed to making
your computer responsive to your needs. CE offers a wide variety of
cross-platform software products aimed at improving your
productivity. Our mission is to continue to delight you with quality
software, documentation and service.
If we can do better, we invite you to tell us.

THANK YOU!

We value you as a customer and want to thank you for your business. We hope you will be pleased with your purchase and would like your feedback. Please don't hesitate to call or write us.

Please remember to fill out your warranty card and return it promptly to DOVE Computer. The card is used to register your name in our automatic update service.

Thanks again from the
Employees at DOVE Computer

CE SOFTWARE

The *axiom* promise ...

Welcome to the new 3rd Edition of the axiom catalogue. We've changed the format quite considerably from the previous editions to reflect the things that you – our customers, have asked us for. We have expanded our product range to include all the products you told us you wanted. From Spreadsheets & Databases to Utilities & Games, the new Software Store section at the back of the catalogue contains all of your favourite software at big discounts off list price – still with the same axiom commitment to excellence in support and service.

We have always put service – looking after our customers – ahead of all other priorities. That is the axiom promise. We are a small company offering a very personal and dedicated service and we promise to give you value for money and personal attention. Whether you need a box of disks or the latest graphics programme, we offer you one-stop shopping and good prices. Nothing is too much trouble for us when it comes to giving you the service you need, and should you have any problems, you can be sure that we'll be on hand to sort them out. Quickly, efficiently – no fuss, no drama. At axiom, your needs come first. That's the way we believe it should be. That's the way it is.

I hope you like the changes we have made – and I hope you like the things that remain the same.

Tim

Tim Felmingham

THE AXIOM CATALOGUE

- What are your reactions to each of the documents?
- What other kinds of goods or services could such documents be used with?
- Would customers in your country like to receive documents like these?
- What are the advantages of ensuring customer satisfaction and encouraging customer loyalty?
- Why is customer loyalty important to a firm?
- What other methods can be used to promote customer satisfaction and loyalty?

2 *Work in pairs* Draft a similar document for a product you're familiar with (or your own firm's product).

8.6 Monday morning: After-sales problems

Work in pairs or small groups Discuss each of these problems and decide how you can solve them. In each case imagine that it's Monday morning …

A You work in the BUYING DEPARTMENT of Rodent International.

1 Read this message which the machine shop supervisor has left on your desk:

> The HD 440 tooling and cutting machine that we bought from Fox Industries Inc. last year has been causing a lot of trouble. We had a service visit last month and before that it was working fine. Now it's making a lot more noise, there's a lot of vibration, it's going slower and worst of all the accuracy is no longer satisfactory. Please contact Fox and get their man to call a.s.ap.

You complained to Fox Industries a week ago about their service on another machine. Here is the letter you sent their Export Sales Manager:

May 20, 1999

Dear Mr Reynard,

As you know, we have bought several machines from your company and been quite satisfied with their performance. We have even recommended Fox machines to other companies. Recently, however, the standard of your after-sales service has got much worse.

Our two HD 55Cs were installed in 1992 and your regular twice-yearly service together with our own maintenance programme has kept them in perfect working order. When there was a breakdown, your service agents used to send an engineer at 48 hours' notice. Now the situation has changed and the engineer promises to come "in about 10 days" and is unable to tell us exactly when he will be arriving. Last week he arrived at 4 pm on Friday afternoon and our own maintenance engineer was unable to leave work until your man had finished.

Let me say that we are not satisfied with this state of affairs. We have already spoken to your service agents about this, but there has been no change so far.

We look forward to hearing from you and hope that you can promise an immediate improvement in your after-sales service.

Yours sincerely,

2 Decide what action you should take in this situation.

3 Draft a suitable letter or fax – or make notes for a phone call.

4 Compare your draft or notes with another pair or group.

5 When you have done this, look at File **76**. Follow the instructions there.

B You work in the SALES DEPARTMENT of Rodent International. Read these faxes from two of your customers.

Decide what you're going to do in each case. Draft suitable letters or faxes – or make notes for phone calls.

You assured us that the equipment would be modified for conditions in this country. We have found that the hardware doesn't work on our voltage, which is 110 volts, 60 cycles.

   Please supply us with suitable transformers by air-freight or replace the equipment with a modified version. Alternatively, we can obtain the transformers locally at your expense.

   Please reply immediately with your decision.

> The equipment seems to be working smoothly after the installation problems. Unfortunately, my works manager informs me that the handbook sent with the machine has got wrongly bound. Apparently, pages 25—50 are missing and 1—24 are included twice!
>
>   Please send us a replacement at once by airmail or courier.

C *Work in groups* Discuss these questions:

- How do you, as a customer, deal with bad service or after-sales service?
- Suppose someone complained about your service or after-sales service: how would you deal with this?
- Does anyone in the group have any 'horror stories' of cases of particularly bad after-sales service?

"Here's your problem – the batteries are in upside-down."

9 Visitors and travellers

9.1 Did you have a good journey?

(A) *Work in pairs* Look at the illustration and discuss these questions:
- What is each person doing? What is going to happen next?
- Have you ever been in any of the situations shown? Tell your partners about your experiences.
- When was the last time you travelled to another country (or another part of your own country)? What did you do there?

(B) ◎◎ 🔊 Here are some phrases which can be used when meeting or being met. Listen to the conversation and highlight the phrases you'd like to remember:

> Hello, are you Mr/Ms ___? I'm ____
> Welcome to ____
> It's a great pleasure to meet you.
> I've been looking forward to meeting you.
> How was your journey/flight?
> I think we'll go to your hotel / our office first ...
> ... my car's outside / we'll take a taxi / we'll take the airport bus.
> Can I take (one of) your bags? Can I help you with your luggage?
> I'll just find a trolley / a porter for your bags.
> Is there anything you'd like to do before we ...?
> Would you like a drink or something to eat before we ...?

> Sorry I'm so late – there was fog at Schiphol / an engine failure outside Cologne / a traffic jam north of Florence.
> I hope you haven't been waiting too long.
> Before we set off, I'd like to have a coffee/beer/sandwich.
> I'd just like to make a quick phone call, if that's all right.
> Very smooth / Not too bad / Pretty tiring / Absolutely exhausting!

C 🗣️ *Work in pairs* Imagine that one of you is a foreign business person arriving at your local airport and the other is waiting to welcome you. Role-play the whole scene, right up to leaving the airport.

Then change partners and role-play the scene again.

D *Work in pairs* Look at these situations and decide:

- WHO would you speak to in each case to get the information you require?
- What EXACTLY would you say in each situation?

Look at the phrases in the speech balloon below for some ideas.

1 You've heard that flight BZ 431 is delayed.
2 You want a rail ticket to Manchester.
3 You want to reconfirm your seat on flight TR 998.
4 You want a plane ticket to Bangkok.
5 You're in a hurry to get to the airport.
6 You've arrived at the airport 3 hours before your flight.
7 You have 3 minutes before your train leaves.
8 You've heard that the 17.55 train has been cancelled.

> *I'd like to reserve a seat on flight number GJ 414 to Toronto.*
> *I'd like to change / reconfirm my reservation on flight number AR 770 on the 16th of this month.*
> *One business class / economy class return / single to Melbourne, please.*
> *Which platform / track / gate does the 13.40 to Glasgow leave from?*
> *Can you tell me what time flight number SQ 060 is due to arrive / depart?*

E *Work in groups* Problems sometimes arise when people are away from home. Discuss these problems with your partners and decide:

- What ACTION would you take in each situation?
- Who would you speak to?
- What EXACTLY would you say to that person?

1 You arrive in good time at the airport but discover that you have lost your ticket. The ticket clerk says your name is not on the computer.
   'Could you check again, please? My name may not be spelt right on the computer. If you still can't find it, could I speak to your supervisor, please?'

2 You find that your travel agent has entered the wrong check-in time on your itinerary and you have missed your flight. Your hosts are meeting you at the airport but by now they will be on their way there.

3 You are a non-smoker but the only seat available on the plane is in the smoking section. After take-off you find that your neighbour is a chain smoker and he doesn't speak English.

4 You arrive at an airport in a foreign country expecting to be met but there is no one there to meet you. You have a meeting in a couple of hours in the centre of the city.

5 Your train has missed the connection and now you're going to be an hour late for your appointment. You have only five minutes to find a phone and make one call.

6 You're seeing off a visitor. You arrive at the airport for his/her flight home and discover that the check-in desk for his/her flight is closed. You go to Airport Information. They tell you that that airline is on strike.

➡ In some cases you may think 'It all depends …' – but what exactly does it depend *on*?

F *Work in pairs* Here is some advice which might be given to travellers. Decide:

- Which of the advice would you recommend to someone who is coming to *your* country?
- Which of the advice would you *yourself* follow when visiting a foreign country?

◆ Photocopy the information page of your passport (the one with your picture on it) and store it in a safe place in case your passport is lost or stolen.

◆ Avoid unnecessary physical contact with strangers. If you are pushed, check your belongings immediately.

◆ Keep valuable documents out of sight.

◆ Keep your passport, tickets and other important documents with you.

◆ Use traveller's cheques not cash.

◆ Never agree to transport anything for a stranger.

◆ Keep your hotel key with you when you leave the hotel, if possible.

◆ Find out which parts of the city are unsafe at night and avoid them.

◆ Walk confidently, as if you know exactly where you're going to.

➡ Add some more advice you would give a foreign visitor to your country. Then join another pair and compare your ideas.

9.2 Hotels and accommodation

A If you have to make a reservation at a particular hotel you know of, you can just send them a fax to book a room:

FAX from   Harry Meier
Acme International Geneva Switzerland   + 41 22 731 91 91

To: Hotel Concorde, Toulouse, France   +33 61 95 78 76

Could I please book three single rooms with bath for the night of Monday 1 April. We shall be arriving at approximately 20.00 hrs.

Please confirm by return.
Many thanks,

Vera Müller
p.p. Harry Meier

But if you require more information about the hotel, or if you have special requirements, you may need to telephone them …

◎◎ You'll hear Ms Müller phoning the Hotel Concorde on behalf of Mr Meier. Note down the answers to these questions about the call:

- Why did she phone instead of sending a fax?
- What information did she get from the hotel?

B *Work in pairs* Imagine that your company is going to send you on a business trip to South America. A colleague has recommended the Rio Othon Palace Hotel and the Caesar Park Hotel.

Rio Othon Palace Hotel

Caesar Park Hotel

1 One of you should look at File **21**, the other at **50**. You'll be calling one of the hotels to book a room.

2 Do the role-play again, with reversed roles.

3 Draft a fax to the hotel confirming the reservation you made on the phone.

C *Work in groups* What kind of hotel would you prefer to stay in if you were on a business trip? How is a business hotel different from a holiday hotel?

Design a new business hotel: the first of a new chain, catering for *mid-budget* business travellers.

1 Decide on the basic concept of your 'product':

- Atmosphere: 'large, streamlined and modern' or 'small, traditional and intimate' – or a new concept …?
- Location: city centre, out of town or in a quiet side street?
- What kinds of people do you want to come to your hotel?
- The staff: will there be a high ratio of staff to guests or will there be an emphasis on self-service?
- What facilities will you offer? Make a list. Here are some ideas to start you off:

  buffet-style breakfast   cocktail lounge   24-hour coffee shop
  fitness centre / gym   free car parking   good towels
  jacuzzi & sauna   photocopying   24-hour room service
  fax phones in every room   hotel secretary   self-service cafeteria
  swimming pool   video movies   fresh fruit and flowers in bedrooms
  restaurant serving local specialities

  + your own ideas: ....

2 Arrange the facilities you have listed in order of importance. Then decide which you will offer – remember that offering every one of them would price your product out of the mid-budget market!

3 When your group has designed 'the perfect business hotel', describe your product to another group or to the whole class.

9.3 Local knowledge: You are the expert!

To a foreign visitor, YOU are the expert on the place where you live. A visitor may expect you to know how to get to places and to explain local customs and habits.

A **1** ◎◎ **at•** Here are some phrases you can use when giving directions. Listen to the recording and highlight the ones you think are most useful.

> You can take the tram – it's the number 89 which says 'ZOO' on the front. You'll need to get a ticket from the machine before you get on. At the fifth stop you get off and cross the road and walk on for about 100 metres. The restaurant is on the left, you can't miss it.

> It's a bit complicated, I'd better show you on the map.
> It'll take about 20 minutes on foot.
> Go to the right as you leave this building and turn left when you get to the town hall.
> Keep straight on and go across the river. You'll see the railway station on your right / on the right.
> Continue along that road for three blocks till you come to a church.
> Opposite the church there's a big square. The restaurant is down a little back street on the other side of the square.

> Drive straight on until you see blue signs that say 'CITY'. Follow these signs as far as the lake and then turn right and drive along the lake for about 5 kilometres. The restaurant is on the right just after the first village, you can't miss it.

2 🗣 *Work in pairs* Play the roles of HOST and VISITOR.

The Visitor needs to know how to get to all the important parts of *your* town or city. Draw a rough street plan before you start – or the Host could draw the map for the Visitor as he or she explains how to get to each place.

➡ Change roles so that you both have a turn as Host.

B It's a good idea to think about how your own country looks from a foreign visitor's point of view. As a resident, your own view may be quite different.

1 *Work in pairs* How much do you know about your own city? Can you answer these questions:

- Where could a visitor go on a free day, or at the weekend?
- When are the museums and art galleries open?
- How can a visitor get tickets for a concert or show?
- Where can a visitor rent a car?
- Which restaurants serve typical local dishes?
- Where can a visitor buy local specialities to take home?
- Where does the bus to the airport leave from and how long does it take?

Join another pair and compare your ideas.

2 *Work in pairs* Imagine that you'll soon be welcoming two people from the other side of the world, who haven't left their own country before. They're coming to work with you for a few months.

Make a list of customs and habits that might seem strange and which might be different from their country. What will you explain to them about ...

- eating – popular dishes, meal times, etc.
- public transport – how do you get tickets, for example?
- shopping – where to buy groceries and clothes cheaply
- work – what kind of clothes to wear, office hours, etc.
- entertainments – where can you go dancing, for example?
- sports – where can you play tennis, work out, swim, etc.?

Form a group of four with another pair Take it in turns to imagine that the others are the newly-arrived foreigners, who need to be briefed on habits and customs in your country.

Change roles so that you all have a chance to be 'foreigners' and 'residents'.

3 Make a list of some famous local names: people who are well-known in your country but may be less well-known abroad.

> 2 national politicians
> 2 local politicians
> 2 historical figures
> 2 TV personalities
> 2 movie stars
> 2 entertainers or artists
> 2 big names in local industry or commerce

Join one or two other pairs Explain to your partners why the people who are on your list but not on theirs are well-known – imagine your partners are foreigners who are unfamiliar with your country.

9.4 Eating, socializing and telling stories

A **1** 🎧 You'll hear two people looking at this dessert menu. What does the man decide to order? What would you order?

DESSERTS

Apple Pie with ice cream, frozen yogurt or fresh cream

Boston Indian Pudding with ice cream, frozen yogurt or fresh cream

Hot Fudge Sundae

Zabaglione

Pecan Pie with ice cream, frozen yogurt or fresh cream

Mississippi Mud Pie with ice cream, frozen yogurt or fresh cream

Pumpkin Pie with ice cream, frozen yogurt or fresh cream

2 🗣 *Work in pairs* Imagine that you're in a restaurant with a foreign visitor who can't understand some of the items on the menu. Play the roles of visitor and host.

➡ IF POSSIBLE, GET A MENU FROM A LOCAL RESTAURANT – or start by composing a menu of your own national dishes.

> *Can you tell me what ...... is?*

> *These are starters, these are main*
> *courses, and these are desserts.*
> *It's a speciality of this region. It's a*
> *sort of ...*
> *That's something rather special. It's a*
> *kind of ...*
> *Well, that's difficult to explain. It's a*
> *bit like ...*
> *I'm afraid I don't know what that is.*
> *I'll ask the waiter/waitress.*

> *That sounds very nice. I'll have that, please.*
> *I don't really like the sound of that.*
> *I'd like to have ...... to start with, followed by ...*

B Preparation

Work alone If you're having a meal or a drink with someone or travelling together, you can't spend all your time talking about business. Much of the time you'll be chatting or socializing. An important part of socializing is telling people about things that have happened to you – unusual, amusing or interesting experiences you've had.

➡ You should do this Preparation at home BEFORE the lesson.

1 Think of three stories you can tell. Think of an amusing, frightening, surprising or embarrassing experience you have had ...

... on a journey by car, plane, train or bus
... in a hotel
... while having a meal
... while meeting or looking after a visitor
... at work

If you can't think of any of your own personal experiences you could retell stories you have heard other people telling – maybe as if they really happened to you.

Make notes to help you to remember the main points.

2 🗣 Here are some expressions you can use when exchanging stories. Highlight the ones you'd like to remember.

> *I'll never forget the day ...*
> *Did I ever tell you about ...?*
> *I had an interesting experience the other day ...*
> *The worst journey I ever made was ...*
> *I had a surprise / I had a fright the other day when ...*

> *That's interesting!*
> *Good heavens!*
> *Good grief!*
> *How embarrassing!*

> *That's amazing!*
> *Good heavens!*
> *How awful!*
> *How terrifying!*

> *What happened then?*
> *What did you do then?*
> *How did you feel then?*

> *Why did you do that?*
> *What did you say then?*

9.4 Eating, socializing and telling stories

C 🔘🔘 You'll hear two people talking about travel experiences. Put the pictures for each story in the correct order – but be careful because some of the things shown in the pictures *didn't* happen!

D Look at the pictures below: they can be interpreted in many different ways.

1 *Work in pairs* Imagine that it is the story of a day that *you* spent travelling – can you work out what happened? Use your imagination to add plenty of details (about the meals and the people you met, for example).

2 When you're ready, join another pair and tell them your version of the story. You could perhaps begin like this:

My car was in the garage being repaired on the day I had to travel to …

and maybe you could finish like this:

… and when I finally got back to my room I wrote some letters and went to bed.

E *Work in small groups* Now it's time to tell your own stories, using the notes you prepared before the lesson. You will probably find, once you get started, that your partners' stories will remind you of other experiences you have had. If so, tell these stories too.

Imagine that you and your companions are business associates. You're sitting together at the end of a meal, just finishing your dessert …

➡ When you're telling a story, it may be a good idea to EXAGGERATE a bit and invent details to make the story more exciting or interesting!

9.5 Organizing a conference

Work in small groups Imagine that you're organizing a weekend conference for about 50 delegates, from the evening of Friday 22 May to lunch time on Monday 25 May. Four foreign speakers have been invited and you'll need to write to them in English.

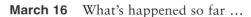

First of all

Discuss what arrangements you'll have to make for the conference. Make a list of the things you will have to do.

Then work through the activity following the instructions below.

March 16   What's happened so far ...

You have provisionally booked 30 double and 10 single rooms at the three-star Hotel du Lac. This hotel has a hall for up to 75 people and three seminar rooms that hold 30 people each. The conference will consist of lectures (in English) in the hall and simultaneous seminars for smaller groups in the other rooms. Four foreign guest speakers have provisionally agreed to take part: their lectures will be on the Saturday in the main hall.

So far, 10 weeks before the conference, you have 23 firm bookings from delegates and 14 provisional ones ...

Draft a letter to the foreign speakers, to include these points:

- Confirm dates and venue of the conference.
- Ask for title and 100-word summary of their talk.
- Explain the accommodation arrangements:

  ```
  You will have sole occupancy of a double room with a view of the
  lake. Your accommodation and full board will be paid for by us.
  ```

- Explain about expenses:

  ```
  We will refund your expenses by cheque in our currency.
  ```

- Ask them to book APEX tickets, not standard fare, as it's over a weekend.
- Make the hotel and the conference sound attractive.

➡ Show your draft letter to another group and make any amendments you think are necessary.

March 30

❶ ⏺️ Now, two weeks later, the four speakers have been in touch with you. They each have special requests. Highlight the important points that each one makes.

> *Mr Santini phoned to say that he thought he was getting a fee for the talk and not just expenses. I said you'd phone him or send a fax today.*

> For the lecture I will need an overhead projector.
>   Will there be photocopying facilities on site?
>   I am not very happy about the hotel arrangements. I would prefer more luxurious accommodation than the conference hotel. Could you book me into a five-star hotel instead, please?
>   Regards,
>
>   *Thomas Brinkmann*

I've decided to bring my family over for a week. During the conference I'll
stay in the hotel but my family will need accommodation for the weekend and
then for the four of us for the week after the conference (till May 30).
Can you find us a 3-bedroom self-catering apartment near the lake?
   Thanks for your help.
   Looking forward to seeing you in May,

Janet Hennessy

◎◎ And you'll hear a recorded message from Madeleine Tennant, the fourth
speaker, which she left on the answerphone early this morning. Note down what
she wants.

2 Discuss with your partners how you will deal with each request, bearing in mind
these points:
- You haven't budgeted for any speaker getting a fee.
- There is a four-star hotel, the Bellevue, about 1 km from the conference hotel,
  but each speaker is getting a very nice double room with a view of the lake at the
  conference hotel.
- Holiday apartments in the village cost £300–400 per week.
- You can only pay expenses in cash if you know the exact amount in advance.
  (The speaker should phone or fax when he or she knows how much the tickets
  will cost.)

3 Draft letters or faxes to each speaker, answering their queries.

➡ Show your drafts to another group and ask for their comments.

April 13

1 Now it's time to send out the programme of the conference. Decide when each of
the speakers will be lecturing on Saturday 23 May:

9.00–10.30	11.00–12.30	14.00–15.30	16.00–17.30

2 Draft a letter to the four speakers, giving this information:
- Tell each speaker when they will be speaking.
- Give details of their accommodation:

   We've booked you a nice room with a balcony overlooking the
   lake. There's a marvellous view of the mountains when the
   weather is clear.

- Give instructions on how to get to the hotel from the airport or station:

   When you arrive at the Airport get a rail ticket to A____ and
   take the train that goes to the Main Station. Change there to a
   local train going to D___ (platform 14 every half hour). A____
   is the 7th stop. The Hotel du Lac is right opposite the station.
   The journey takes about one hour.

- Say that you're looking forward to meeting them and that there will now be
  about 70 delegates.

➡ Show your draft to another group and ask for their comments.

Follow-up   Join another group and discuss what you did in this activity.

10 Marketing

10.1 The marketing mix

A *Work in pairs* Make a list of seven products (goods and services) that are produced or provided in your city or region.

Victoria State Opera

Make the right decision about your business career.

VICTORIAN BUSINESS COLLEGE

ACCOUNTING

MARKETING

INFORMATION TECHNOLOGY

SECRETARIAL STUDIES

BUSINESS TRAINING

Victorian Business College
A U S T R A L I A

a local brand of drink ....
a grocery product (breakfast cereal, health food, etc.) ....
an industrial product (machines, consumer goods, vehicles, etc.) ....
a place of entertainment (theatre, cinema, etc.) ....
a public service (telephones, mail, transport, etc.) ....
an educational service (maybe the course you're doing now?) ....
another well-known local product ....

B *Work in groups* Discuss these questions about some of the products you've listed:
- What competition does each product face?
  (The competition may not be another brand, but another type of product: people may prefer to spend their spare cash on clothes instead of going to the cinema, for example.)
- What is the image of each product?
- What is the image of the company that produces it?
- How strongly or weakly is each of the products marketed?
- Where is each product advertised?

C *Work alone* Fill the gaps in the sentences below with words from this list.

commercials   competes   design   distribution   end-users   hire purchase
image   labels   mail order   materials   newspaper advertisements
opportunities   outlets   place   posters   price   product   promotion
public relations   radio spots   rival   satisfy   strengths   threats   weaknesses

1 **What is 'the marketing mix'?**

The marketing mix consists of 'the four Ps': providing the customer with the right
P _____ at the right P _____ , presented in the most attractive way
(P _____) and available in the easiest way (P _____).

2 **What is 'a product'?**

A product is not just an assembled set of components: it is something customers buy
to s _____ a need they feel they have. The i _____ and the
d _____ of the product are as important as its specification.

3 **What is 'price'?**

The product must be priced so that it c _____ effectively with
r _____ products in the same market.

4 **What is 'promotion'?**

The product is presented to customers through advertising (e.g. TV
c _____ , r _____ , n _____ , p _____), packaging
(e.g. design, l _____ , m _____), publicity, P.R. (_____)
and personal selling.

5 **What is 'place'?**

Your product must be available to customers through the most cost-effective
channels of d _____ . A consumer product must be offered to
e _____ in suitable retail o _____ , or available on
h _____ or by m _____ .

6 **What is meant by 'S.W.O.T.'?**

A firm must be aware of its S _____ and W _____ and the
O _____ and T _____ it faces in the market place.

D *Work in groups* Which of these opportunities and threats do firms in your region face
in the next two to three years?

Competition from other local firms, or from other regions
Rise or fall in demand
Changes in customers' tastes and buying habits
Higher wages and salaries
Customers becoming more price-conscious, or more quality-conscious
Cheaper, or better quality, imported goods
New technology

➡ What are these local firms' STRENGTHS and WEAKNESSES?

10.2 Advertisements and commercials

Preparation

Cut out two of your favourite advertisements from a magazine or newspaper – you might like to cut out one ad you *hate* as well, perhaps!

Prepare a short presentation of each advertisement so that you are ready for step **C** at the end of this section.

> Promoting a product involves developing a 'Unique Selling Proposition' ('USP'): the FEATURES and BENEFITS which make it unlike any of the competing products.
>
> There are four stages in promoting a product ('AIDA'):
>
> 1 attract the ATTENTION of potential customers
> 2 arouse INTEREST in the product
> 3 create a DESIRE for its benefits
> 4 encourage customers to take prompt ACTION

A You'll hear two people talking about one of the ads on the next page. As you listen, look at the questions in **B** below:

- Which questions did the speakers NOT deal with?
- Which of the points they made do you disagree with?

B *Work in pairs* Study the advertisements on the next page and discuss these questions:

- What exactly is the product being 'sold'?
- How well does each ad succeed in the four stages of 'AIDA' (see above)?
- What kind of customers is each advertisement directed at?
- What is the 'Unique Selling Proposition' of each product?
- What changes would have to be made to the style or tone of the ads to make them suitable for your country?
- Which is the 'best' ad, do you think? Why?

C *Work in groups* Show the ads you have cut from magazines and newspapers to the members of your group.

Present each one to the group, covering these points:

- ◆ Target customers
- ◆ The USP of the product: its features and benefits
- ◆ How the ad works in terms of the four stages of 'AIDA'
- ◆ How the style would have to be changed for other markets

At the end, when everyone has presented their ads, decide which is the best one, and why.

➡ What are your favourite TV commercials? Describe them to your partners and explain why you think they are effective.

> I'd like to show you an ad that really impressed me.
> What do you think of this ad? It shows ...
> This ad seems to be aimed at ...
> According to this ad, the USP of this product is ...
> What I don't like about this ad is ...

Relieve tense nervous headaches fast.

You need to choose… ?

BEN & JERRY'S®

VERMONT'S FINEST · ICE CREAM & FROZEN YOGURT™

UNITED COLORS OF BENETTON.

WHERE WOULD YOU BE WITHOUT OUR TRAVEL GUIDES AND MOTORING MAPS? OUR RED GUIDES DESCRIBE MORE HOTELS AND RESTAURANTS THAN ANY OTHERS. OUR GREEN GUIDES MARK PLACES·OF·INTEREST WITH ONE, TWO, OR THREE STARS. OUR MAPS ARE UP·DATED EVERY YEAR AND THEY'RE ALL CROSS·REFERENCED. SO YOU CAN MOVE EASILY FROM ONE TO ANOTHER. MAKE SURE IT'S A MICHELIN. YOU'LL BE ALL OVER THE PLACE WITHOUT US.

WHERE TO STAY

WHAT TO SEE

WHERE TO GO

MICHELIN MAPS AND GUIDES

Relieve tense nervous headaches fast.

First Choice Holidays

10.3 Promoting products and brands

Promoting a product doesn't only involve advertising, it involves considering it as a 'Total Product': its brand name, presentation, labelling and packaging are all part of the total product – as well as its instructions, reliability and after-sales service. A service is also a product and customers must be made aware of what is being offered.

A *Work in pairs* Choose some of the products shown above and discuss these questions:
- Which of the following methods are used to promote each of them?
- Which methods would probably not be suitable?

**brochures   catalogues   leaflets   packaging   direct mail
point of sale displays   press releases   showrooms
stands at trade fairs and exhibitions   sports sponsorship   word of mouth**

B ◎◎ You'll hear part of a lecture. The speaker is talking about brand names that sound strange or comic to British ears, or which were changed for the British market.

Mark the brand names with a tick ☑ if they are on sale in the UK, or with a cross ☒ if they are not on sale in the UK under that name.

Portable radios: Party Center   Concert Boy   Party Boy
    Yacht Boy

Drinks: Pocari Sweat   Calpis   Pschitt   Sic
    Irish Cream liqueur   Irish Mist liqueur

Food: Bum bubble gum   Mother biscuits   Bimbo bread
    Häagen-Dazs ice cream

Cars: Cedric   Gloria   Bluebird   Applause
     Accord   Carina   Previa   Micra   Corolla
     Primera   Pajero   Ranchero   Shogun   Mondeo   Celica
     Xantia   Vauxhall   Opel   Astra
     Kadett   Nova   Corsa   Rabbit   Golf
Computer software: Pagemaker   Page Maker   PageMaker
     Word perfect   Word Perfect   WordPerfect
     Quark Express   QuarkXPress   Quark XPress
     MicroSoftWord   MicroSoft Word   Microsoft Word

C **1** *Work in pairs* Here are ten global brands:

Mercedes-Benz

Can you name ten well-known brands which are their competitors?
Name another five famous global brands. What products are they connected with?

2 Here are five famous luxury brands. What are they famous for? Why do people pay
so much money for these brands?

3 *Join another pair* Compare your answers to the questions. How important are
well-known brand names for you personally?

10.3 Promoting products and brands

If you're certain about something you can simply say:

> *It will happen* or *It won't happen*
> *It's true* or *It isn't true*
> *It happened* or *It didn't happen*

If you're uncertain you can simply say:

> *It may happen* or *It might happen* or *It could happen*
> *It may be true* or *It might be true* or *It could be true*
> *It may have happened* or *It might have happened* or *It could have happened*

But in many situations you'll probably want to express your meaning more precisely – or maybe more emphatically.
You may want to show the DEGREE OF PROBABILITY:

100% probability:	75% probability:	50% probability:	25% probability:	0% probability:
Certain	**Likely**	**Possible**	**Unlikely**	**Impossible**

A 🔘 You'll hear some colleagues talking about a sales campaign. Write in their names below, to show how certain each of them is.

1 Was all the sales literature sent to Toronto?

certain (100%)	likely (75%)	possible (50%)	unlikely (25%)	impossible (0%)
Betty.......	Diana.......	Alan........	Christian..	Eric.........

2 Is the new sales drive in Canada going to succeed?

certain (100%)	likely (75%)	possible (50%)	unlikely (25%)	impossible (0%)
....	....	....	....	....

3 Will the new product range make a big impact on the Canadian market?

certain (100%)	likely (75%)	possible (50%)	unlikely (25%)	impossible (0%)
....	....	....	....	....

4 Were the sales forecasts for Canada encouraging?

certain (100%)	likely (75%)	possible (50%)	unlikely (25%)	impossible (0%)
....	....	....	....	....

B 🔊 Here are some useful phrases that can be used when talking about possibility, probability and certainty:

100% **I'm sure that** these sales figures are accurate.
The figures **must be** accurate.
There's no doubt that the figures were carefully checked.
The figures **must have been** thoroughly checked, so **I'm absolutely sure that** they're accurate.

75% Our sales in the USA **are likely to** go up next year.
I expect that our sales in Canada will go down.
I wouldn't be surprised if our sales in Mexico went up.
It's quite possible that our sales in Peru will go up.
Our sales in Argentina **may well** remain static.

50% **There's a chance that** we'll manage to break into the UK market.
It's just possible that your forecast is over-optimistic.
I'm not sure if the figures I've noted down are accurate.
There may have been some kind of mistake.

25% Singapore **probably isn't** a very profitable market for us.
I don't think that we'll be able to sell in Japan.
Thailand **is unlikely to be** a good market for our product.
I doubt if we'll be able to make any sales in Korea.

0% **I'm quite sure that** it isn't worth appointing an agent in Zambia.
Sales in Tanzania **can't have been** worse than they are now.
Uganda **definitely isn't** a good market for our product.
These figures **couldn't possibly be** accurate.

C 🔊 *Work in pairs* We asked a number of business people to predict events they thought might happen in the next twenty years or so.

Listen to what they said and discuss each prediction with your partner. Say how likely you think it is that each event will happen. Use the expressions from **B**.

D *Work in groups* Marketing often involves spotting trends and deciding what may happen next in the market place.

Pick some of these products and imagine that you are marketing them. What trends do you foresee in the next few years?

sport and fitness
holidays
air travel
restaurants
banking
shops and stores
cars
computers
home entertainment
your own firm's product
(or a product you know about)

In this activity you will be deciding how to market a product you're very familiar with – your own region.

Japan...Where the past greets the future

A *Work in pairs* Look at the statistics below. How much of this information is relevant to marketing your own region? Imagine that your customers are likely to be British or American – or people who would otherwise go to the UK or USA.

Annual number of foreign visitors (millions)

	from all countries	from UK	from USA
Australia	3	0.3	0.3
Austria	19	0.7	
Canada	15	0.6	12.0
France	53	7.4	
Germany	45	1.8	
Greece	9	1.6	
Ireland	4	2.4	0.4
Italy	20	1.2	1.8
Japan	4	0.2	0.6
Mexico	7	0	5.5
Spain	55	6.6	
Switzerland	13	1.1	1.0
Thailand	6	0.3	0.3
UK	19	–	2.7
USA	46	2.8	–

Annual number of foreign visitors (millions)

from	to the USA	to the UK
Australia	0.5	0.5
Canada	17	0.6
France	0.7	2.5
Germany	1.2	2.3
Ireland	0.1	1.4
Italy	0.4	0.8
Japan	3.2	0.6
Mexico	6.8	0
Netherlands	0.3	1.0
Spain	0.1	0.7
Switzerland	0.1	0.4
UK	2.7	–
USA	–	2.8
ALL visitors	46	19

Amount spent on travel abroad in US dollars per head

	US $
Americans	$170
Australians	$230
Austrians	$835
British	$230
Canadians	$340
Dutch	$515
French	$220
Germans	$500
Italians	$230
Japanese	$195
Spanish	$115
Swedes	$725
Swiss	$990

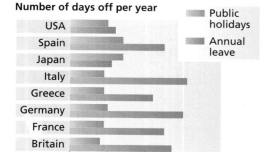

Number of days off per year — Public holidays, Annual leave (USA, Spain, Japan, Italy, Greece, Germany, France, Britain; scale 0 10 20 30 40)

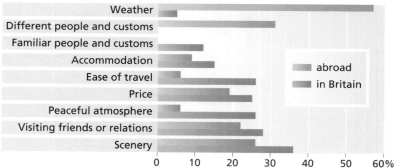

Reasons why British people spend their holidays in Britain or abroad — abroad, in Britain (Weather, Different people and customs, Familiar people and customs, Accommodation, Ease of travel, Price, Peaceful atmosphere, Visiting friends or relations, Scenery; scale 0 10 20 30 40 50 60%)

➡ Compare your ideas with the rest of the class.

B *The class is divided into three groups* Group A should look at File **23**, group B at **53** and group C at **77**.

① Each group designs a questionnaire about the region and its competitors and then conducts interviews with consumers (i.e. potential visitors).

② When your group has designed its questionnaire, each member of the group should stand up and go round the class finding 'members of the public' (from other groups) to interview. Ask each of them the questions in your questionnaire.

[If possible, this should be continued out of class, with the questions translated into your own language if necessary.]

③ Report back to your group. Make a simple table using the information you have collected.

④ Each group reports its results to the whole class.

Make notes on the important points made by the other groups. Ask questions on any points they haven't made clear.

or

Form new groups of three, consisting of one member from each of the original groups. Find out what each of the groups discovered.

⑤ *Work in groups* Each group should consist of one member of each of the original groups. Decide together:

- Who are your (potential) customers?
- What are the main 'features and benefits' of your product?
- What are the main 'features and benefits' of the competition?
- What is the 'unique selling proposition' that makes your product special?
- How can you inform customers about your product?
- What positive points about your region should you stress?
- What misconceptions about your product should you try to correct? For example, if people think your region is 'flat and boring' or 'hot and dangerous', how can you persuade them they're wrong?

⑥ *Work as a whole class or in two large groups* Devise a marketing strategy for your product. How can you improve your product's image and promote it to the customers?

⑦ Think of a good slogan for your product. If you had to choose one photo to illustrate the product, what would it show?

Write a short text for an advertisement in an English-language newspaper or magazine.

C *Work in groups* Discuss these questions about the activity in **B**:

- What important processes were missing from the activity?
- Which of the processes really require specialist skills from outside agencies or consultants?
- What are the differences between marketing a region and marketing …

    an industrial product   a consumer product   a service?

- 'Marketing is just sales with a college education' – to what extent do you agree?

11 Meetings

11.1 Taking part in a meeting

A *Work in pairs* Look at the pictures and discuss these questions:

- What seems to be happening in each illustration? What do you think the people might be talking about?
- Which of these meetings would you feel most comfortable taking part in? Give your reasons.
- Which of them is most *unlike* the meetings you have attended? Why is this the case?
- How long do you spend in meetings in an average week?

B *Work in pairs* You'll hear the beginning of one of the meetings illustrated above. Imagine that you work for ACME Trading, the same company as the speakers: the heads of department are discussing a proposal to introduce flexible working hours ...

Mr David Brown (chair)   Mrs Carla Baldini   Mr Alex Bergman   Mr Ron Johnson
   Miss Anna Maria Garcia   Mr Enzo Rossini   Ms Tina Legrand

1 ◎◎ Listen to the recording and tick ☑ the points in this list that the speakers make.

> Most people are happy with the present system. ✓
> With flexitime some people would benefit more than others. ✓
> Any department can decide not to adopt flexitime. ✓
> 'Core times' from 10 to 3 are too restrictive. ✓
> The staff canteen must be open longer at lunchtime – say from 11.30 to 2.30.
> Staff should be able to build up 'credit' by working longer, so that they can take extra days off – i.e. 'flexible days' as well as flexible hours. ✓
> Each department should set its own core times, according to its busiest times of day. ✓
> Flexible hours should only be worked on Mondays and Fridays.
> Every department should work to the same core times. ✓
> Staff should be allowed to work all through the lunch hour and not have a lunch break.
> 'Flexible days' would be very confusing for visitors and callers. ✓

2 Discuss these questions with your partner:
- How was this meeting different from meetings you've attended?
- How well did the chairperson control the meeting?
- In what ways was the meeting different from an informal discussion?

3 **ab** Here are some expressions that are often used in meetings. Highlight the ones you think are most useful.

If you're in a meeting, you can find out what the other people in the group think by saying:

> What are your views on this, John? Do you agree, Mary?
> Mr Brown, what do you think about this? Ms Smith, what's your opinion?

If you want to interrupt someone and put forward your own opinion you can say:

> If I could just make a point here ... Could I make a suggestion?
> Sorry to interrupt, but I'd just like to say that ... It seems to me that ...

If you want to find out if the others in the group have understood or if they agree with you, you can say:

> Do you see what I mean? Are you with me?
> Don't you agree, Simon? Are we unanimous?
> Don't you think so, Mrs Robinson? Does anyone object?

If you don't understand what someone has said, you can say:

> Sorry, could you say that again, please? Sorry, I didn't quite understand.
> I'm sorry, I didn't catch what you said. Sorry, I'm not quite with you.

4 ◎◎ Listen to the recording again. You'll hear many of the expressions being used in the meeting.

C *Work in groups* Imagine that you work in one of the departments at ACME Trading. As you heard in **B**, a system of flexible working hours has been proposed. Now each department is holding a further meeting to discuss how to proceed. Bear in mind the management's stipulations and what other members of staff have suggested.

Management stipulations:

· Only certain days in the week should be designated 'flexi-days'.
· There should be a period of 'core time' when every full-time member of staff is in the office.
· At all times, between 9 and 5 telephones have to be answered and visitors need to be received.

Suggestions from members of staff:

I don't mind working longer hours, provided that the hours are 'credited' later.

The rush hour traffic is getting worse and it takes all of us too long to get to work in the mornings - and home again in the evenings.

I would like to be able to leave earlier on Thursday or Friday to do my shopping.

If there was a 'pairing' system, you'd always have someone else to cover for you in your absence.

As a part-time worker, I would prefer to work most of my hours in the mornings.

I want to take my children to school in the mornings and pick them up in the afternoons.

I would prefer to start work at 10 on Mondays.

1 Decide who is going to chair your meeting and then hold the meeting. Work out a set of proposals which will satisfy everyone. At present your office hours are Monday to Friday nine to five (with an hour for lunch).

2 *Join another group* Find out what another department's proposals are. Then discuss these questions:

• What did you find most difficult in the meeting?
• How well did the person in the chair control the meeting? Did everyone have a chance to put forward their points of view?
• If you were going to do the activity again, what would you do differently?

D *Work in groups* Discuss these questions:
• What 'golden rules' can you suggest to make sure meetings are successful?
• What advice would you give to someone who feels too shy to speak their mind at meetings?

11.2 One-to-one meetings

A ◎◎ *Work in pairs* You'll hear the beginning of a one-to-one business meeting. Pam Ross has called to see Paul Fisher in his office. After you have listened to the recording, discuss these questions:

• What was the purpose of the meeting?
• What do you think happened at the end of the meeting?
• How was it different from a social meeting between friends?
• How was it different from the meeting you heard in **11.1B**?

Starting a meeting

> Hello, thanks for agreeing to see me.
> Hello, it's good of you to come and see me.
> It's good to see you again.
> Shall we get down to business?
> There are a few questions I'd like to ask: ...

Ending a meeting

> Well, I think that covers everything.
> I think that's about all for the time being.
> So do we agree that ...?

> I'll put these proposals in writing and fax them to you tomorrow.

B *Work in groups of four   Each group should consist of TWO PAIRS* You'll be role-playing a meeting between a client and a salesperson discussing the idea of using your school, college or institution as a venue for a seminar or conference.

1 Spin a coin to decide which pair will play the role of salespeople (Pair A, who are 'selling' the venue) or clients (Pair B, the conference organizers).

2 Pair A Decide how well your college can cater for a seminar or conference. How many participants can be comfortably accommodated in the premises? What facilities can you offer? How will you deal with accommodation for the delegates?

   Pair B Make a list of the requirements you have for your seminar/conference. What facilities will you require?

3 [icon] Phone the other pair to confirm or discuss the arrangements for the meeting.

4 Pair A Draft an agenda for the meeting.

   Pair B Draft a list of questions you will ask the salespeople.

5 [icon] One member of Pair A goes to meet one member of Pair B to have a one-to-one meeting. Imagine that, like Ms Ross and Mr Fisher in the conversation you heard earlier, you already know each other, and you haven't met for quite a while.

   Make notes as you go along on the decisions you reach.

   The other member of each pair will be sitting in on the meeting and making notes as 'Observers'. They should NOT participate in the meeting.

   If you're an Observer, note down ...
   • what the client and salesperson did well
   • what they did less well
   • what they forgot to do
   • what you would do differently
   • any other comments on their meeting

6 At the end of the meeting the Observers give their feedback.

   Also, compare the notes the client and salesperson made: did they note down the same points?

7 Change roles and hold the meetings again, so that the Observers can themselves receive feedback as client and salesperson.

11.3 Different kinds of meetings

A You'll hear part of a one-to-one meeting between two managers, Kate Thomas and David Williams. First, read the agenda Kate sent David for their meeting:

to David Williams

AGENDA FOR MEETING ON APRIL 4

Guidelines for people who travel abroad on our behalf, arising from J.L.'s trip to Germany & F.E.'s trip to Japan

Advance to cover anticipated expenses:
• How much should the advance be?
• When should it be paid?
• How should they pay their on-the-spot expenses when abroad?

Air travel:
• Who should book & pay for the tickets?
• Who should check dates & times?
• What class: club (business) or economy?

Itinerary:
• Who should have copies of it?
• What details should be on it?

Accommodation:
• What kind of accommodation should we book?

Any other business

1 🔘🔘 Listen to the recording and note down the conclusions that are reached on each point on the agenda above.

2 Compare your notes with a partner. Then discuss these questions:
• What were the differences between this internal meeting about travel arrangements and the meeting between a supplier and customer you heard in **11.2 A**?
• How was this meeting different from a social meeting between friends?
• What impression did you get of the effectiveness and efficiency of the meeting? Give your reasons.
• How would the meeting have gone differently if more people had been involved? What if J.L. and F.E. had themselves been present at the meeting?

B *Work in small groups* Look at the eight problems on the next page. What kind of meeting is the best way of dealing with each one?

a) a one-to-one meeting of two of the people involved
b) a meeting of four or five of the people involved
c) a meeting of about ten of the people involved
d) a meeting of everyone involved
e) no meeting: one person should decide what to do and then inform everyone by phone or by sending out a memo

1 A large, influential customer continually pays late. Your sales manager and credit controller have politely and repeatedly complained but this hasn't made any difference. The time has come to decide what to do about this.

2 In a small factory the older workers are ignoring safety rules and encouraging the younger ones to do the same. Some of these rules may be excessively cautious and the older workers' production rates are very good.

3 In a medium-sized factory, groups of workers operate as teams. One group has been getting poorer results than the other teams and verbal warnings have had no effect.

4 The firm is having a bad year and it will probably be necessary to make five members of the office staff redundant. The normal policy is 'last in – first out'.

5 Someone has been leaking information about your firm's products to your competitor. It may be a member of your staff or one of your preferred suppliers.

6 The board requires a report on your department's long-term plans over the next ten years.

7 The territories covered by your sales force have been unchanged for ten years. A revision of the boundaries might make the team more efficient.

8 There is to be a company picnic next month and everything has to be planned and organized.

Discuss the alternatives like this:

> *If you had a meeting of four people, the others might think that ...*
> *If the manager sent everyone a letter, everyone might ...*

C *Work in groups* Imagine that you are members of a Staff Committee investigating ways of improving working conditions in your offices. After the meeting your proposals will be submitted to a Management Committee.

1 Decide who will be 'in the chair' and who will take the minutes and note down your proposals. Before the meeting starts, the chairperson should look at File **80**, the others at Files **24, 54** or **78**.

2 Hold the meeting.

3 Approve the list of proposals made by the person who took the minutes.

D Now imagine that you are members of the Management Committee who have been sent the list of proposals (written by one of the *other* groups, not your own).

1 Decide who is to chair your meeting and who will take the minutes. Before the meeting starts, the chairperson should look at File **80**, the others at Files **25, 55** or **79**.

2 Hold the meeting to discuss the proposals you have received.

E *Work in pairs* Role-play a one-to-one meeting between a manager and a staff representative to discuss the Management Committee's proposals.

11.4 We need to have a meeting ...

A 🔊 *Work in pairs* You'll hear some business people talking about things that can go wrong at meetings. Discuss these questions:

- Which do you think are the worst things the speakers mention?
- How can these problems be avoided?
- Which of the things they mention don't usually happen in your experience – or don't really matter?

B You will be holding a meeting to organize ...

A SOCIAL EVENT
– a company picnic, a departmental party, a group social evening or a class excursion.

1 *Work as whole class* First of all, draft an agenda to include some or all of these points – and add more points that need to be covered in the meeting:

- ◆ the date and duration of the event
- ◆ what form it should take
- ◆ who will be invited
- ◆ transport arrangements
- ◆ catering
- ◆ who will be responsible for organizing it
- ◆ how the preparation work will be shared
- ◆ any other business

Each proposal should be a separate item on the agenda.

2 *Form two large groups* Both groups will be following the same agenda – later you'll be able to compare what happened. Agree when the meetings should both end. Decide who's going to chair your meeting. (The chairperson should look at File **80** for some tips.)

3 Hold the meeting. Everyone, apart from the chairperson, should MAKE NOTES on the decisions that are reached.

If time runs out before the meeting has reached its conclusions, the meeting should be adjourned (to be continued after class, perhaps).

Here are some more expressions that you can use in this meeting:

> **What does everyone think about this?**
> **Let's put this to the vote.**

> **I suggest that ...**
> **I propose that ...**

> **I agree with that suggestion because ...**

> **I don't quite agree with that point because ...**

> **I think it's time to adjourn the meeting.**
> **I think we're running out of time.**

> **Is there anything else we should discuss?**
> **Is there any other business?**

---

4 *Work in pairs* Compare your notes with another member of your own group. Make sure that you have noted all the important points.

5 *Work in pairs with someone from a different group* Using your notes, tell your new partner what happened at your meeting. What are the differences between the decisions your two groups reached?

6 Draft a report of the meeting. Summarize your discussion and record the decisions that were reached. Include details of the time, date and duration of the meeting, and the people who were present.

C *Work in pairs* Look at these opinions about meetings. Put a tick ☑ beside the opinions you share and a cross ☒ beside the ones you disagree with.

'Oh no, not another meeting!'

We asked some business people for their opinions. Here's what they said ...

1 The purpose of most meetings is to decide when the next one will take place.

2 A meeting is a group of people who can decide nothing alone and who decide together that nothing can be done.

3 It's better to send everyone a memo about a new procedure than to have a meeting about it.

4 Meetings help everyone to feel personally involved in decision-making.

5 It's better for the boss to make a decision than to have a meeting.

6 The most important person at a meeting is the chairperson.

7 The most important piece of paper at a meeting is the agenda.

8 Most meetings are unnecessary, they're just a way of making people feel important.

9 It's better to talk to each person individually than to call them all together for a meeting.

10 A meeting may be the only chance the members of a group actually have to see each other face-to-face.

11 Meetings lead to better decisions, because of the exchange of information and ideas.

12 You can never rely on the person who takes the minutes to tell the truth about what actually happened at a meeting.

13 More time is wasted during meetings than during any other business activity.

➡ *Join another pair* Compare your answers. Discuss any of the other pair's views that you disagree with.

"Mr Jepson said that while I was sending out for coffee he would like a hamburger. Mr Willis said that he thought he would like a hamburger, too, medium with no tomato. Ms Lester said that that sounded good and that she would like a hamburger, too, rare with a side of French fries. Mr Anderson said that if everybody else was going to have something to eat he might as well have a meatball sandwich and a piece of apple pie. Mrs Colby said she'd like a slice of anchovy pizza and a bag of Fritolays ..."

12 Processes and operations

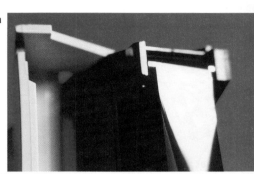

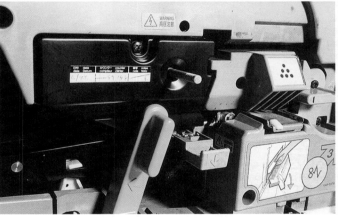

A *Work in pairs* Look at the pictures and discuss these questions:

1. What are the products shown in the photos?

2. Which of these products do you know how to use? Could you give someone else instructions on how to use it?

3. Can you explain how each one works? What are the principles behind each of them?

4. What is difficult about explaining how something works – apart from knowing the right technical terms to use?

B **①** *Work in pairs* Look at these explanations of how a photocopier works. Then discuss these questions:

- Which of the explanations is the easiest to follow? Why?
- What are the best aspects of each one?

② *Join another pair* Compare your views.

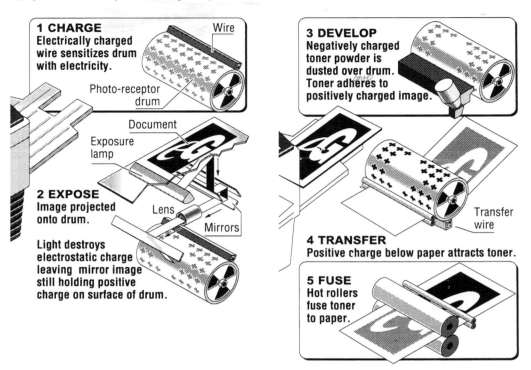

1 CHARGE
Electrically charged wire sensitizes drum with electricity.

Wire

Photo-receptor drum

Document

Exposure lamp

2 EXPOSE
Image projected onto drum.

Light destroys electrostatic charge leaving mirror image still holding positive charge on surface of drum.

Lens

Mirrors

3 DEVELOP
Negatively charged toner powder is dusted over drum. Toner adheres to positively charged image.

Transfer wire

4 TRANSFER
Positive charge below paper attracts toner.

5 FUSE
Hot rollers fuse toner to paper.

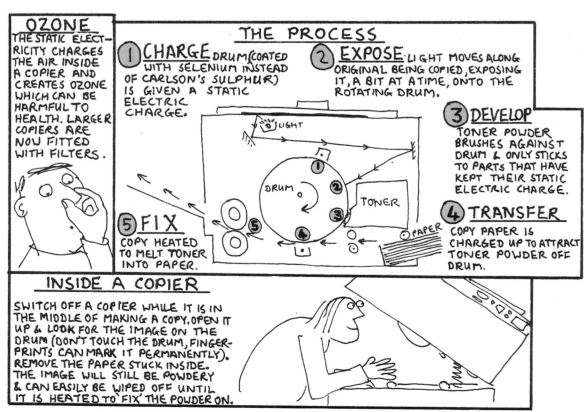

OZONE
THE STATIC ELECTRICITY CHARGES THE AIR INSIDE A COPIER AND CREATES OZONE WHICH CAN BE HARMFUL TO HEALTH. LARGER COPIERS ARE NOW FITTED WITH FILTERS.

THE PROCESS

① **CHARGE** DRUM (COATED WITH SELENIUM INSTEAD OF CARLSON'S SULPHUR) IS GIVEN A STATIC ELECTRIC CHARGE.

② **EXPOSE** LIGHT MOVES ALONG ORIGINAL BEING COPIED, EXPOSING IT, A BIT AT A TIME, ONTO THE ROTATING DRUM.

③ **DEVELOP** TONER POWDER BRUSHES AGAINST DRUM & ONLY STICKS TO PARTS THAT HAVE KEPT THEIR STATIC ELECTRIC CHARGE.

④ **TRANSFER** COPY PAPER IS CHARGED UP TO ATTRACT TONER POWDER OFF DRUM.

⑤ **FIX** COPY HEATED TO MELT TONER INTO PAPER.

LIGHT

DRUM

TONER

PAPER

INSIDE A COPIER
SWITCH OFF A COPIER WHILE IT IS IN THE MIDDLE OF MAKING A COPY. OPEN IT UP & LOOK FOR THE IMAGE ON THE DRUM (DON'T TOUCH THE DRUM, FINGERPRINTS CAN MARK IT PERMANENTLY). REMOVE THE PAPER STUCK INSIDE. THE IMAGE WILL STILL BE POWDERY & CAN EASILY BE WIPED OFF UNTIL IT IS HEATED TO 'FIX' THE POWDER ON.

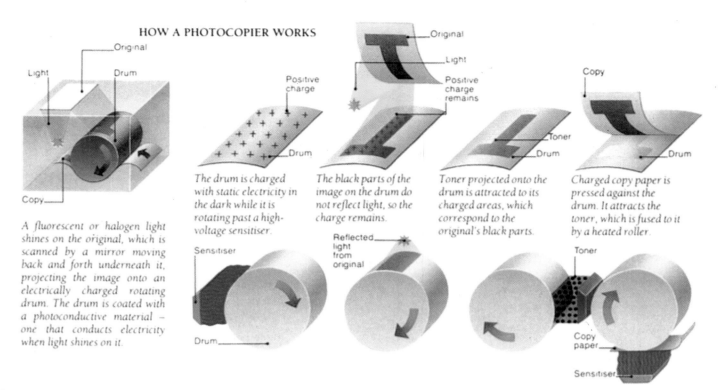

HOW A PHOTOCOPIER WORKS

A fluorescent or halogen light shines on the original, which is scanned by a mirror moving back and forth underneath it, projecting the image onto an electrically charged rotating drum. The drum is coated with a photoconductive material – one that conducts electricity when light shines on it.

The drum is charged with static electricity in the dark while it is rotating past a high-voltage sensitiser.

The black parts of the image on the drum do not reflect light, so the charge remains.

Toner projected onto the drum is attracted to its charged areas, which correspond to the original's black parts.

Charged copy paper is pressed against the drum. It attracts the toner, which is fused to it by a heated roller.

C ◎◎ You'll hear someone explaining the same process. He makes a good job of this – but he makes THREE mistakes. Note down the mistakes he makes.

D *Work in groups of four or five* Two of you should look at File **26**, and the others at File **56**. You'll see an explanation of how a fax machine or a hard disk works. Later you'll have to explain how it works in your own words.

12.2 What do I have to do?

A 🔘🔘 You'll hear explanations of how to operate three products.

1 Listen to each conversation and decide what each product is. How long did it take you to work it out?

2 Listen to the first and second conversations again. Note down the four main points that are made in each explanation.

B Look at these expressions which are used when explaining a procedure.

at🔘 Highlight the ones you think are most useful.

To explain the order in which certain things are done:

> First of all ...
> The next thing you have to do is ...
> ... And then finally ...

To add a further point:

> Make sure you ...
> Oh, and by the way, don't forget to ...
> Oh, and be careful not to ...

To check that the other person is following you, or has understood:

> OK, so is that clear?
> Does that seem to make sense?
> So there we are. Do you have any questions?

If you want to ask someone to explain something to you, you can say:

> Excuse me, could you show me how to ...?
> I wonder if you could tell me how this works?

If you haven't understood the explanation, or if you can't follow the instructions, or if you want to check that you've understood so far, you can say:

> I'm sorry, I didn't quite follow you there.
> I'm sorry, what did you say that part was called?

When you think you've understood, you can say:

> If I've understood right ...
> So is the basic idea that ...?
> You mean ...

C *Work in pairs* One of you should look at File **62**, the other at File **68**. You'll have to explain to your partner how to draw a continuous line in this box, using the letters and numbers as your 'reference points'. In the end your continuous line will have created a picture!

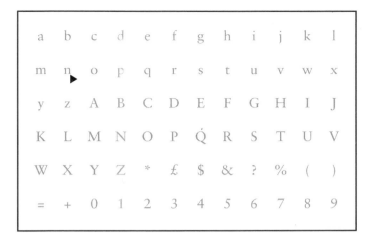

First of all, draw a straight line from ...
When you reach capital B ...
Then carry on down till you come to ...
Draw a curved line between ...
Now continue the line as far as ...
Pass round number 8 and then ...

D ❶ *Work in pairs* Look at this flowchart which shows the process of booking a ticket for a flight. These three steps have been left out: decide which of the boxes they fit in.

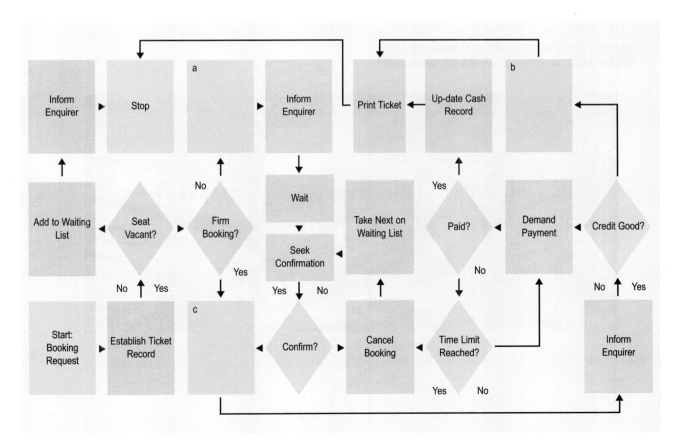

② *Work in pairs* Run through the steps in the flowchart together, 'talking it through' as you help each other to understand the procedure.

③ *Form a pair with a different student* Imagine that one of you is a new employee in a travel agency, the other a more experienced member of staff. Go through the procedure for taking a booking, using the expressions presented in step **B**.

E *Work in pairs* Explain to your partner how to operate another machine or gadget, or how to carry out a process or an operation.

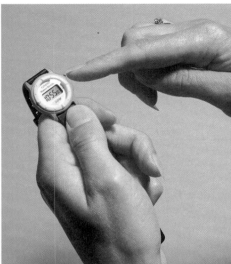

12.3 A production process

Cadbury Limited

A *Work in pairs* Ask your partners what they already know about chocolate manufacture and discuss these questions:
- How is chocolate produced?
- Which of these items are ingredients of chocolate?

    cocoa   coffee   sugar   fat   milk   vitamins   tea   eggs   malt
- How does chocolate get its characteristic taste and texture?

B ◎◎ *Work in pairs* You'll hear an expert explaining how chocolate is produced and the various operations involved in its manufacture. Listen to the recording.

1 Look at the flowchart of the process and number the operations in the blue box below, according to the recording.

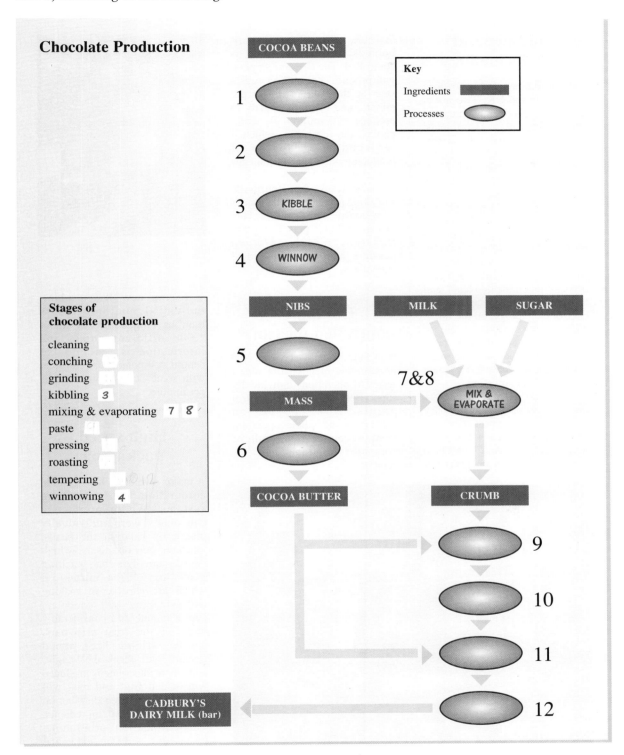

Chocolate Production

COCOA BEANS

Key
Ingredients
Processes

1

2

3 KIBBLE

4 WINNOW

NIBS   MILK   SUGAR

5

7&8

MIX & EVAPORATE

MASS

6

COCOA BUTTER   CRUMB

9

10

11

12

CADBURY'S
DAIRY MILK (bar)

Stages of chocolate production

cleaning ☐
conching ☐
grinding ☐
kibbling *3*
mixing & evaporating *7* *8*
paste ☐
pressing ☐
roasting ☐
tempering ☐
winnowing *4*

2 Which of the stages apply to the actual chocolate production process? Which apply to the preparing of the ingredients?

C *Work in pairs* Now read the description of the latest production developments.

1 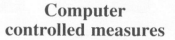 Highlight the expressions which are used to describe the new plant in a POSITIVE way.

Cadbury and New Technology

Cadbury operate three chocolate factories in the UK. Two are at Bournville producing chocolate bars and chocolate assortments; the other, the Somerdale factory, produces bars such as *Double Decker*, *Crunchie* and *Fry's Turkish Delight* which are known as 'countlines'.

The modernization programme at Bournville, begun in 1980, has involved the rationalization of production. This consisted in bringing together individual product processing, on the one hand, and the most modern processing and control technology, on the other. The specialist machinery comes from Britain and abroad and a number of these machines have been produced to Cadbury's own design and specification.

The new plants operate 24 hours a day producing Cadbury products to the highest standards of quality control. The new *Wispa* plant produces 1,680 bars per minute with such precision that the size of the tiny air bubbles in the chocolate is controlled. The *Creme Egg* plant will produce 300 million eggs a year at the rate of 1,100 per minute, and has the capacity to produce 370 million. By comparison the machinery which it replaced was capable of producing only 257 million eggs annually.

Each week the Bournville site alone produces 1,500 tonnes of chocolate – 1.6 million bars of various kinds plus 50 million *Hazelnut Whirls*, *Almond Clusters* and other individual chocolates.

Computer controlled measures

Before the automation programme, manufacture was a series of operations individually supervised at separate control points. Now one person supervises the whole operation from a control room full of computer terminals and TV screens.

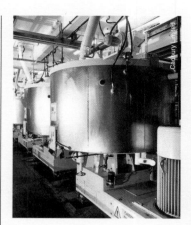
Conching tank

In the new *Wispa* plant, individual microprocessors monitor temperature at about 1,000 different points and information is fed into the central computers that can deal with some 360,000 instructions per minute.

High speed packaging

A major revolution has been the automation of the packing systems. Where previously chocolates were individually placed by hand in the boxes, machines now do this. New high speed chocolate bar packing plants have been introduced which are capable of making and wrapping 800 chocolate bars a minute and considerably more of the treat size bars. These variable high speed systems will check the weight, and where chocolate is produced with added fruit and nuts will also check for even distribution of these additional ingredients. The automation programme means that a dozen individual manufacturing plants will have replaced 37 old plants.

One of the central control rooms

2 What is the *most* positive aspect of the process from the point of view of the company, do you think?

3 Now read the passage once more and mark whether the statements below are true ☑ or false ☒:

1 The Bournville factory produces the countlines. ☐
2 The specialist machinery is produced by Cadbury. ☐
3 The size of air bubbles in the chocolate is precisely controlled. ☐
4 The old machinery could only produce 257 million eggs annually. ☐
5 Chocolates are no longer individually packed. ☐
6 Individual microprocessors control temperature changes. ☐
7 The packing systems check the weight of the additional ingredients. ☐

D *Work in groups* Discuss whether what you read about in **C** represents the future for all manufacturing processes. Consider these questions:

1 What advantages and disadvantages do you see with the introduction of more automated plants?
2 Can you agree on areas where you think it is a good idea to use them?
3 What will industrial workers then do?
4 Is it the end of work, as we understand it? And the beginning of The Leisure Society?
5 What do you think about training people to work in such plants?
6 Who decides what should be made? What is your opinion of this?
7 What are the advantages of manufacturing processes where only one person is needed?
8 What prospects do you see for the spreading of such operations and processes in your country?

E Think of a service or manufacturing process you know about. Write a description of how it works, together with a flowchart, if possible.

12.4 When things go wrong ... What do we do?

17 May 1999

Breakdown leads to bottleneck

Delta Tools were yesterday unable to meet their daily deadline. After a sudden, inexplicable breakdown at their Southford site the main assembly line was put out of action. Components from supplying firms continued to be delivered, but despite determined attempts to utilize all the available space the plant was soon brought to a halt. The late shift had to be sent home

Work in pairs Imagine you work for a multinational manufacturing company at one of its European plants. You are the personal assistants of the Chief Executive Officer. There have been a number of delays and breakdowns in production recently which have been reported in the press. You have been asked to consider what steps can be taken to prevent the same problem happening again.

1 What happened, according to the newspaper report? Now read the consultant's report and the internal memos below. Highlight key sections and try to agree what really happened.

2 Take notes and draft a report to your European regional director explaining what happened.

Industrial Research Consultants Inc.

Buffalo Grove Il 60090 USA
. . . .

Consultant's Report
April 5, 1999

You have a wide range of equipment on the site at this point, as you can see from the attached drawing. All available space has to be utilized. So we must restrict the number of materials which are actually present at any given time. Clearly if a particular component is not available when it is required on the assembly line that might lead to a hold-up. In most production units you will, of course, have bottlenecks. But we should not allow any gaps to occur, if possible. The latest conveyor technology is clearly required.

A further point concerns production time. The machines do not operate night and day at the moment and the operators work a two-shift system at present. We are hoping to put forward a plan to streamline production in the coming months. Once we have solved the technical problems – and our designers are currently working on a project to modernize your handling equipment – all the facilities in the plant will be co-ordinated to enable you to step up production of the new range of products.

Unfortunately, as you know, there has been a major problem with reorganizing the maintenance schedule. In the past two years standby crews were on duty around the clock. But

Memorandum

From: Chief Executive
To: Production Director

April 10, 1999

This is a great idea, Ralph. Please investigate fully automated handling equipment and the possibility of installing new robots for finishing and assembly shops. Also make sure the recommendations of the consultant are put into practice.

3 *Join another pair*
Compare notes and read the report they have drafted.

INTERNAL MEMO

FROM: Production Director
TO: Personnel Director   April 15, 1999

John. As you know we're working under great pressure in all departments at the moment to keep up the output for the export and US orders. The new jobs are needed badly. All our maintenance staff are extremely overworked.

Can you please readvertise the vacant jobs for the additional maintenance engineers and the five new technicians. Things cannot go on as they are now. We're badly understaffed. One day the new robots are going to break down, when the line is not covered by the service department. You know how much we need people with all-round electronic and mechanical qualifications so that the wide range of machines we operate are fully supervised at all times.

We must introduce a three-shift system for the maintenance people. They never have time to put the faults right at the moment. You should emphasize the large bonus payments for working unsocial hours and nights

13 Jobs and careers

13.1 The ideal job?

A *Work in pairs* Look at the photos and discuss these questions:
- What would you enjoy about each of the jobs?
- What would you dislike about each job? Why?
- What are the most important things for you in your work? Arrange these aspects in order of importance and add some more things you think are important:

> job satisfaction   meeting people
> earning plenty of money   earning enough money
> having pleasant co-workers/colleagues   security

- Out of all the people you know, who has the job you'd most like to have? Why?
- If you could choose any job in the world to do, what would it be? Why?

B *Work in pairs* Read this newspaper article and find the answers to these questions in the text:

1 What were the TWO reasons why Virgin Atlantic was considering redundancies?
2 What were the TWO things Richard Branson invited his staff to do?
3 How many people volunteered to take unpaid leave?
4 How did the long break affect the staff's attitude to their work?
5 Why is the scheme attractive to new recruits?
6 Is the scheme going to become permanent?

FRONTIERS OF WORK

Branson's new route to more jobs

Celia Weston

FOR many young people lucky enough to get a job after leaving school or college, the biggest shock of the transition to work is how few holidays they get.

Having spent their academic years working an eight or nine-month year, it can be depressing to realize that for the rest of their working lives they will be able to take only four weeks off a year.

Many would jump at the chance to take three months off – and that's exactly what happened at Virgin Atlantic, the airline run by Richard Branson. He believes the new initiative could help to reduce unemployment.

Faced last autumn with the recession and with its failure to acquire more flight slots out of Heathrow airport, the company was having to consider redundancies. Mr Branson wrote to staff saying that cutting back on jobs was "something I have never wanted to do". Instead he invited employees to take up to six months unpaid leave and to participate in a job sharing scheme.

The immediate crisis passed but the idea of a shorter working year took off. When the company later asked for 300 volunteers to take three months unpaid leave, 450 put their names forward. Mr Branson said: "To be fair and share it around, in some cases we said that people could only take six weeks."

Most of the volunteers were cabin crew but other staff, including secretaries and pilots, took advantage of the offer as well. "And when they came back from their break ... they definitely seemed to enjoy work more," he said.

The company tends to recruit and train its own staff from scratch. As Mr Branson said: "If you've been at college or on the dole, working for only nine months still makes you a lot better off financially than you were before." He believes there is a broader social benefit to be achieved. "If you are only taking on people for nine months, that will enable others who would otherwise have no work or be living on the dole to have a chance too."

And he goes further. "I think this should be the basis of a pattern across the whole European Community for the first few years of working life."

Nor was a shorter working year only applicable to young people. "If older women and men with children can afford it because one partner's working 12 months and the other nine, I think a lot of people would like to earn slightly less and be able to spend more time with their children," Mr Branson said.

This year the scheme is on offer again, although not over the busy summer period. "All the people who took time off last year would like to do so again," Mr Branson said. But its realization depended on whether the company could recruit enough people to allow 400-500 existing staff to take three months off.

The company was considering whether the arrangement should become a permanent feature, Mr Branson said. "For new people being taken on in most departments, we're thinking about making nine-month working a standard contract."

C *Work in groups* Discuss these questions:
- What are your views on Richard Branson's scheme? Would you like to participate in such a scheme?
- Would such a scheme succeed in the firm you work / have worked for? Why not?
- Why do you think so many of Virgin's cabin crew took advantage of the scheme?
- Could this kind of scheme only succeed with a youthful staff who have few family responsibilities?
- How could you persuade people who have considerable working experience and are used to earning a certain wage that they should take a pay cut?
- What do you think of the following:

    a four-day week   a nine-day fortnight   seasonal work   job sharing

13.2 Applying for a job

A *Work in pairs* Discuss these questions:
- What impression do you try to give in an application letter?
- Should an application letter be handwritten, typed, or laser-printed?
- How important is a well-presented CV or résumé?
- Do you always tell the absolute truth in application letters?

B **①** *Work in pairs* Look at this job ad: what would be its attractions – what might be its drawbacks?

WORK IN BERMUDA!

ACME Atlantic are a well-known and respected trading company. We handle imports directly from manufacturers in 35 different countries, often to our own specifications, and currently export to 46 different countries worldwide.

We are looking for enthusiastic people to work in our office in Bermuda on temporary 3-, 6- and 9-month contracts. Applicants must be able to speak and write at least one foreign language fluently and can be nationals of any country.

Experience in import/export will be an advantage, but as special training will be available this is not essential. The main requirements are a willingness to work as a member of a team, to cope with pressure, to use the telephone in a foreign language and in English and to be prepared occasionally to work long hours when necessary.

There are several posts available and long-term prospects are good, though initially all successful applicants will be contracted for a maximum of 9 months.

The salary we will offer is excellent. We will pay for your return air fare and provide adequate accommodation at a nominal rent.

Please apply in your own handwriting, enclosing your résumé, to Charles Fox, European Sales Office, ACME Atlantic Ltd, 45 Pentonville Road, London EC2 4AC.

② *Work in pairs* Look at this résumé. If you were interviewing Kevin Willis for the job in Bermuda, what questions would you ask him about his career history?

Kevin Miguel Willis

Address	1090 Madison Avenue Sheboygan WI 53081
Res. phone & fax:	555–5656898
Date of birth:	2/21/71
Professional experience	Aug. 1994–present Valentine International: Export clerk Jan. 1993–July 1994 Chicago Products: Marketing assistant May 1992–Dec. 1992 Self-employed: travel guide Jan. 1992–May 1992 Unemployed
Education and training	1988–1990 Green Bay High School, Green Bay, Wisconsin
	1986–1988 Oshkosh Junior High School, Oshkosh, Wisconsin
Interests	Mountain biking, reading, hiking, skiing, sailing
Languages	Fluent Spanish (my mother is Mexican), good conversational French
References	Ms Daphne Stern, Sales Vice-President, Valentine International, 2205 Jackson Street, Oshkosh, WI 54901 Mrs Francine Dexter, Marketing Director, Chicago Products Inc., 4450 Capitol Drive, Milwaukee, WI 52303 Mr James Wong, Atlas Travel, 9004 South Michigan Avenue, Chicago IL 60607

③ *Work in pairs* Look at this application letter from another applicant for the job. In what ways does Arthur Dent seem suitable (or unsuitable) for the job? In what ways are YOU better qualified for it?

Dear Mr Fox,

<u>Work in Bermuda</u>

I noted with interest your advertisement in today's Daily Planet.

You will see from the enclosed CV that I have three years experience in marketing. My responsibilities have included all types of administrative work, product development, arranging and attending presentations, working with clients and solving problems that arise.

Although I have an excellent relationship with my present employers, I feel that my prospects with them are limited and that there would be more scope for my talents with a larger, more dynamic company.

If you consider that my qualifications and experience are suitable, I should be available for interview at any time.

Yours sincerely,

Arthur Dent

④ *Work in pairs* Imagine that you want to apply for the job. Draft an application letter, following these guidelines:

1 Introduce yourself: name, age, nationality, etc.
2 State when you are available.
3 Describe your relevant experience — or justify your lack of experience.
4 Describe your skills in your own language, English and other languages.
5 Describe how you meet the requirements of the job.
6 Say when you're available for interview.

C Read this article. What are your reactions to it?

Too old at 30

I'M CONTEMPLATING applying for my fifty-first job. It's been a long time since I wasted stamp money this way. In fact, when I reached the fiftieth without success I decided to abandon job-hunting and got out my pen to scratch a living instead.

But there's another wildly exciting job in the paper today, "salary £12,500–£16,250 according to age and experience". The good news is the pay, the bad news is that damning little phrase "according to age and experience" which means I won't get the job.

It's not that I have more age than experience – I've led an incident-packed existence. Unfortunately it's not all related to a single-strand career structure. Journalist, temp, company director, wife and mother, market researcher, and now, at thirty-something, I'm trying to use my Cambridge degree in criminology.

I'm a victim of the sliding pay-scale. Employers can obtain a fresh 22-year-old graduate to train a lot cheaper than me. Yet I'm the ideal employee: stable, good-humoured, child-bearing behind me, looking for 25-plus years of steady pensionable employment.

Ageism is everywhere. It's much more prevalent than sexism in the job market, or that's how it seems from where I'm standing. Even the BBC is a culprit. Their appointments brochure says: "The BBC's personnel policies are based on equal opportunities for all … This applies to … opportunity for training and promotion, irrespective of sex, marital status, creed, colour, race or ethnic origin, and the BBC is committed to the development and promotion of such equality of opportunity. Traineeships … are available to suitably qualified candidates under the age of 25."

Ageism is lagging behind sexism, racism, and handicappism because even the oppressed seem to accept the discrimination. The public and private sectors are obsessed with attracting young high-flyers. Yet there are many professions that would benefit from the maturity and stability the older entrant can bring. This is recognized by the Probation Service, for example, who welcome experienced adults looking for a second career.

The armed services and police, perhaps, could think about strenuous aptitude and fitness tests rather than imposing a blanket upper limit on entrants which is arbitrarily and variously fixed between 28 and 33. The administrative grade of the Civil Service assumes the rot sets in at 32.

My own pressing concern is to alleviate my guilt. I loved every minute of my university education, and I'm desperately grateful to the Government for financing me through this at a cost of over £10,000. But unless someone gives me a job, how can I pay them back in income tax?

JENNY WARD

1 *Work in pairs* Decide whether statements 1 to 10 are true ☑ or false ☒, according to the article.

1 The writer is over forty years old. ☐
2 She gave up applying for jobs some time ago. ☐
3 She has not had much experience of working for a living. ☐
4 Employers think that someone of her age is too expensive to employ. ☐
5 She needs a job so that she can support her family. ☐
6 People don't get as angry about ageism as about other forms of discrimination. ☐
7 Employers are looking for bright, ambitious people of any age. ☐
8 More mature employees would be valuable assets to many professions. ☐
9 People in their thirties can't get jobs in government departments. ☐
10 She wants to 'repay' the State for her university education. ☐

2 *Work in groups* Discuss these questions:
- What would you do if you were in the same position as the writer?
- Do you know someone who is unlucky or unsuccessful in getting jobs?
- Can you explain the reasons for their lack of success?
- What could they do to improve their chances of success?
- How does the law in your country discourage discrimination by employers?

The Council has Nursery facilities available for employees who have caring responsibilities for a child or children aged between 6 months and school age. Also available are dependant care allowances for evening commitments.

We are actively working towards equality of opportunity and welcome applications from any individual.

Waltham Forest serves a multi-racial community and welcomes applications from women, black and ethnic minorities, people with disabilities, lesbians and gay men to help build a representative workforce.

The Liverpool Students Union is committed to the effective implementation of its equal opportunities policy.
Applicants are considered on their suitability for the post regardless of sex, sexual orientation, religion, racial origin, nationality, marital status, disability or age (under 65).
Working with students and the community.

The City Council is an Equal Opportunity Employer and welcomes applications, irrespective of the applicant's race, sex, marital status, age, sexual orientation, religious beliefs, disability or employment status. The City Council is working towards a smoke free environment.

13.3 Interviews

A *Work in groups* Think of the last interview you attended and discuss these questions:
- What was the worst thing about it?
- What difficult questions were you asked?
- Why do you think you were successful, or unsuccessful?
- If you could go through the interview again, what would you do differently?
- In an interview, do you always have to be completely honest?
- What impression do you try to give in an interview?

B ◎◎ *Work in pairs* You'll hear extracts from two interviews. Use this assessment form to decide which candidate performed better on a scale of 1 to 5.

	Sue Jones	Tom Richards
qualifications		
confidence		
reliability		
personality		
work experience		
overall impression		

➡ And which interviewer did the better job, do you think?

C *Work in small groups* Imagine that a young friend of yours is about to attend his or her first interview. Note down some more advice that you would give:

> Do your homework: find out about the company
> Prepare some questions to ask about the company and what the job entails
> Wear smart, formal clothes   Don't smoke
> Arrive a few minutes early   Sit up straight
> Look straight at the interviewer
>
>   Expect the unexpected — and don't panic!

➡ Join another group and compare your notes.

D ◎◎ *Work in pairs* Some interviewers give candidates a hard time by asking them difficult questions – like the 13 questions below. Listen to the recording and discuss these points:

• Can you think of three more questions you might be asked at an interview? Add them to the list.
• What would your own answers to each of the questions be? Rehearse your answers with your partner and make notes.

```
 1   Tell me about yourself.
 2   What do you think are your strengths and
     weaknesses?
 3   We have a lot of applicants for this job, why
     should we appoint you?
 4   Which is more important to you: status or money?
 5   How long do you think you'd stay with us if you
     were appointed?
 6   Why do you want to leave your present job?
 7   What would you like to be doing ten years from
     now?
 8   What are you most proud of having done recently?
 9   What is your worst fault and what is your best
     quality?
10   Don't you think you're a little young/old for
     this job?
11   What are your long-range goals?
12   What excites you about the job you're doing now?
13   How would you rate your present boss?

14

15

16
```

E Work in groups of three Take it in turns to be the Interviewer, the Candidate and the Observer. Allow enough time for each of you to have a turn at being the Candidate.

Interviewer Ask the Candidate the questions you discussed in **D**. Avoid asking Yes/No questions. Perhaps try to give him or her a hard time by asking supplementary questions like these:

Why do you think that?	*In what way exactly?*
Could you explain why you think that?	*What do you mean exactly?*
Can you give me an example of that?	*Are you quite sure you mean that?*

Candidate Do your best to answer the questions and try to keep cool!

Observer As you listen to the interview, make notes on these points:
- What impression did each person give?
- If they were nervous, how did this affect their performance?
- Were there too many Yes/No questions?
- Which questions did they answer badly?
- Which questions did they answer well?
- What advice would you give them for their next real interview?

13.4 The Real Thing

A Work in two large groups Each group should decide on one job that would be attractive and realistic for most of the members of the class to apply for. Perhaps this could be your 'ideal job' – the one you'd immediately apply for if you saw it advertised.

Write an advertisement for the job and, if possible, make copies for the other group to see. Alternatively, pin it to the classroom notice board or stick it on the white/blackboard.

B In this simulation, half the class will be playing the role of INTERVIEWERS and the other half the role of CANDIDATES. Each panel of interviewers works for a firm of consultants, and they will interview several candidates for both jobs advertised.

Decide which members of the class are going to play the roles of candidates, and which are going to be the interviewers. Follow the instructions below, according to your role.

1 **Interviewers** Work with the other member(s) of your panel. Decide what questions you are going to ask each candidate.
- What personal qualities are you looking for?
- Are you going to be kind to the candidates or give them a hard time?

Candidates Choose one of the jobs advertised.

Write a short letter of application for the job. (This letter will accompany your CV, if you have one.)

2 **Interviewers** Read the letters of application and any CVs you receive.

Decide which candidates look promising and what special questions you'll ask each one.

Candidates Work with another candidate and decide what impression you'll try to give.

Look again at the difficult questions in **13.3D** and make sure you know how to answer them.

3 Now it's time for the interviews to take place.

Each interview panel should have its 'office' in a different part of the room. Candidates go to a different 'office' for each interview.

The CONTROLLER will tell you how long is available for each interview and work out a timetable that allows time for panels to see at least three candidates. Each panel must stick to this schedule, so that other panels are not kept waiting.

Interviewers Look at the checklist in File **82**.

Candidates Between interviews you should wait in a separate area – preferably in another room or in the corridor.

4 When the interviews have finished, all the interviewers and all the candidates should meet in separate areas.

Interviewers Tell the other panels about the candidates you have interviewed.

You can recommend up to three people for both posts. Decide which candidates will be short-listed.

Candidates Imagine that you're meeting in a local café. Tell the other candidates how you got on in your interviews.

- What mistakes did you make?
- Which of the panels conducted the best interviews?
- What advice would you give them about their interviewing techniques?

Decide which panels were the best.

5 Now meet again as a class.

Interviewers Announce your short lists of successful candidates.

Candidates Announce which panel you voted 'top interviewers'.

6 *Work in groups or as a class* Finally, discuss these questions:
- How did you feel at each stage of the simulation?
- What did you learn from doing this simulation?
- How did any real interviews you've had compare with this one?
- If you could do the whole simulation again, what would you do differently?

"Number two was reasonably OK. At least he took his Walkman off for the whole of the interview."

14 Sales and negotiation

A *Work in pairs* Look at the photos and discuss these questions.

- What is happening in each picture?
- What do all the situations have in common?
- What are the people saying?
- Have you ever been in any of the situations shown? What was it like?
- What sort of products and services are involved?
- What sort of relationship do the people have with each other?

B Now read this text. Which of the points do you agree or disagree with? Give your reasons.

Anyone who has contact with customers is a salesperson – that includes the telephonist who answers the phone and the service engineer who calls to repair a machine. So that probably includes you!

The relationship between a salesperson and a client is important: both parties want to feel satisfied with their deal and neither wants to feel cheated. A friendly, respectful relationship is more effective than an aggressive, competitive one.

A salesperson should believe that his or her product has certain advantages over the competition. Customers want to be sure that they are buying a product that is good value and of high quality. People in business are not going to spend their company's money on something they don't really need (unlike consumers, who can sometimes be persuaded to buy 'useless' products like fur coats and solid gold watches!).

Some salespeople adopt a direct 'hard sell' approach, while others use a more indirect 'soft sell' approach. Which approach do you prefer? Whichever approach is used, in the end perhaps a good salesperson is someone who can persuade anyone to buy anything. On the other hand, maybe a good salesperson is someone who knows how to deal with different kinds of people and who can point out how his or her product will benefit each individual customer in special ways. After all a buyer is called a 'buyer' because he or she wants to buy. All you need to do is to convince them that your product is the one they want. A successful sales meeting depends on both the salesperson and the customer asking each other the right sort of questions.

14.2 The sales process

A *Work in pairs* Fill the gaps in these sentences with these words:

before   buying   client   individual   product   wants   weaknesses

If you want to be a successful negotiator and salesperson you should …

1 Know your .... and its main features.
2 Know the strengths and .... of competing products.
3 Find out who makes the .... decisions in your client's firm.
4 Plan each sales interview .... it takes place.
5 Match what you're selling to each client's .... and needs.
6 Listen to what your .... tells you.
7 Remember that each client is an ...., not a number.

B ◎◎ *Work in pairs* You'll hear part of a talk at a workshop for people who have little experience of selling. Listen to the recording and answer these two general questions:

1 What is the talk about?
2 What stages are referred to in the talk?

C ◎◎ Listen to the recording again and fill the gaps in this summary of the talk.

1 The   Stage:
   usually a phone call. You have to talk to   in person
   – not his/her   .
   Identify yourself and arrange an   .
2 The   Stage:
   a) prepare and   with a   or   .
   b) dress suitably for the   .
   c) behave in a   , confident but   manner.
   d) don't spend too long on   .

e) show that you're a   ,   person.

f) mention   firms who use your product.

g) tell the client about the   of your product.

h) encourage your client to talk by   and only
    talk   the time yourself.

3 The   Stage:

recognizing exactly when your client is ready to   the order.

This depends on

Finally,   your client for the order and leave.

14.3 Selling your product

A ◎◎ You'll hear a sales representative demonstrating this product to a customer.

1 *Work in pairs* Listen to the recording and then discuss these questions:
- How much attention is the customer paying?
- How convinced is the customer of the camera?
- Which of these aspects is NOT covered in the demonstration:

> advertising   after-sales service   film for the camera
> guarantee period   pricing   using the camera

Note down the QUESTIONS that the customer asks the sales rep.

2 Listen to the recording again. This summary of the points the sales representative makes is jumbled up. Number the points in the order in which he makes them. The first one is done for you:

> 1 *When you look at a Nimslo 3-D print you get an amazing feeling of depth and realism.*
> *We're running a national advertising campaign.*
> *It's not possible to let you have the goods on sale or return.*
> *Special introductory offer: first three films are processed free.*
> *The cost to the end-user will be under £100. Plus the usual trade discount.*
> *It uses normal 35mm film.*

B *Work alone or in pairs* Think of a new product you've recently bought – preferably something that's not too large to take to class with you.

① List the features and benefits of the product.

   e.g.   *It's a ...   It's the latest ...   It can replace ...*
          It's used for ...   Its features and benefits are ...

② Make notes on how it works.

③ Take your product to class and demonstrate it to your group.

C ①  *Work in pairs* Student A should look at File **28** and student B at **83**. You'll be taking part in a meeting between a salesperson and a customer.

② Now student A should look at File **83** and student B at **58**.

14.4 Negotiating on the phone

A ◎◎ *Work in pairs* You'll hear part of a telephone negotiation about the sale of yogurt between a salesperson and a buyer. Note down your answers to these questions:

1 What are they talking about?
2 What significant points were made?
3 Who made them?
4 What do you think the salesperson will do after the telephone conversation?
5 Is the fax below an accurate reflection of the phone call?

North Holland Dairy Cooperative, Volendam, Postbus 4550 NL–4452

Ms Irena Eichelberger
Wholesale Groceries Inc.
P. O. B. 5678
A-1090 Wien
Austria

Dear Ms Eichelberger,

<u>Telephone conversation 29 February 1999</u>

This fax is to follow up our telephone call of this morning.

We are willing to supply 2,000 (two thousand) tonnes of our variety Splendide at $150 (one hundred and fifty dollars) per tonne. We expect to make the delivery at the latest by 15 March.

Jan van Geelen

B [👤👤👤] *Work in groups of three* You are going to take part in a telephone sales negotiation. Student A is the buyer and looks at File **29**, student B is the seller and looks at File **59** and student C looks at File **84** (the 'Observer').

C *Work alone or in pairs* Draft a follow-up fax to the buyer or customer confirming your call and what you agreed on. (The fax in **A** can serve as a model.) Give your fax to another pair to respond to.

14.5 Getting it right in negotiations

A *Work in pairs* You work in the buying department of an electrical appliances manufacturer. You recently bought some cheap electrical components from Coyote Enterprises. The quality seemed to be up to standard …

1 ◎◎ Your boss, Bob Kellerman, is talking to your Sales Manager, Michelle, on the phone. Listen to the call and make notes. Then discuss these questions:

- What do you think has happened?
- What sort of supplier are you dealing with?
- What action should you take in this situation?
- How do you think your boss will deal with it?

2 ◎◎ Listen to the conversation between Bob Kellerman, your boss, and the supplier, Mr Wiley, and make notes on the dispute. Then answer these questions:

- Which points were made?
- Who made these points?
- How would you feel if you were in a situation like the one you've just heard?
- Can such a conflict be solved by negotiation? What might the alternative be?

➡ Decide what further questions you'd ask Mr Wiley …

B **1** *Work in pairs* Read this article and try to agree what the terms *debating* and *bargaining* refer to:

> *A much simplified view of what goes on in a negotiation says that there are Four Main Phases of Negotiation:*
>
> **1** The preparation phase: this is where you work out what you want and which are the main priorities.
>
> **2** The debating phase: during this phase you try to find out what the other side or the customer wants. Say what you want but do not say what the final conditions are yet. Use open questions and listen to your customer. Try to find out in what areas the other side may be prepared to move.
>
> **3** The proposal phase: this is the point at which you suggest some of the things you could trade or which you might be prepared to trade. Formulate your proposals in the form of *if …, then …* . Be patient and listen to the other side's proposals.
>
> **4** The bargaining phase: this is the period or part where you indicate what it is you will actually trade. Here you exchange conditionally in turn particular points, *if …, then …* . Remember to write down the agreement.

2 Answer these questions:

1 When do you use expressions in the form of *if …, then …*?
2 When do you suggest some of the things you might be prepared to trade?
3 Why should you be patient and listen to the other side's proposals?
4 When do you work out what you want and which are the main priorities?
5 What should you not forget to do in a negotiation?
6 What sort of questions should you use in the early phases?
7 Why do you think that is?
8 In what phase do you suggest things you are ready to trade?

C ◎◎ *Work in pairs* You'll hear a face-to-face negotiation taking place between Fritz, a German wholesale buyer of plant-based raw materials for a chain of companies manufacturing organic products, and Marianne, a French supplier.

1 Listen to the recording. First decide which order the following points are mentioned in. Next, decide which points Marianne (M) raises and which Fritz (F) raises. The first is done for you as an example in each case.

ORDER THE POINTS ARE MENTIONED		WHO FIRST RAISES THE POINTS
....	discount	....
....	good price	....
...1.....	competitive prices	...F......
....	guarantees	....
....	importance of quality	....
....	the need for firm figures	....
....	perfect condition	....
....	the point about the organization being flexible	....

2 Listen to the recording again and decide in which phases of the negotiation these words in the box were used in the conversation:

> a) *If there's a guarantee, then we are prepared to …*
> b) *I can let you have orders for at least two hundred tonnes.*
> c) *If we order immediately two hundred in total, with the second hundred deliverable in three months, then …*
> d) *What are you saying, how much?*

Phases of Negotiation:

1 Prepare: what you want ....
2 Debate: what do they want? ....
3 Propose: what could you theoretically trade, offer, concede? ....
4 Bargain: what will you, in actual fact, trade, offer, concede? ....

D **1** 📇 *Work in groups of four (pairs of pairs)* Pair A are the sellers. Pair B are the buyers. You are involved in preparing a sales negotiation concerning an electrical component. Before you start the sales negotiation with the people from another firm decide together what the margins for the sale are going to be. Pair A decides on the seller's limits or margins and looks at File **30**. Pair B decides on the buyer's limits or margins and looks at File **60**.

2 📇 *Change partners* The new pairs consist of a buyer and a seller. Student A looks at File **32**, student B looks at File **61**.

3 *Work in groups* Report on how 'successful' you were in your negotiation.

E *Final discussion* What are your opinions on this American negotiation expert's view:

> *In business you don't get what you deserve, you get what you negotiate.*

14.6 Negotiating an international deal

A ◎◎ *Work in pairs* You'll hear extracts from seven negotiations. Listen to the SECOND speaker in each case. If you encountered each of these people in a negotiation what would you think of them? Make notes.

1 _____

2 _____

3 _____

4 _____

5 _____

6 _____

7 _____

➡ Discuss some of the different behavioural styles in negotiation which you know or have experience of.

B 📇 *Work in two large groups* First decide on one product to sell. It should be a realistic item you are familiar with or would like to sell in your current or future work. Then draft a very brief specification of the product. This is written (or typed and photocopied, if possible) to be used in the next stage of the simulation.

C In this simulation, half the class will be playing the role of SELLERS and the other half the role of BUYERS. Both sides work for firms negotiating with a foreign firm to finalize a deal on the sale or purchase of a product.

Decide which members of the class are going to play the role of SELLERS, and which are going to be the BUYERS. Follow the instructions on the left or right below, according to your role.

1 The SELLERS send a copy of the product and its price and other specifications to the BUYERS.

2 **Sellers** Work with the others in your team. Use the product specification you agreed on. Decide how far you are prepared to move in your specifications and margins, and try and agree as a team on the margins you will be negotiating within.

Decide on a delegation leader or leaders. These will initiate the discussions and speak first in the negotiation sessions. The others will come in and provide support if necessary.

Buyers Read the product specification. Work with the others in your team. Decide how far you can move in your specifications and margins, and try and agree as a team on the margins you will be negotiating within. How far will you go in your demands for price, quantity and delivery dates? How much discount will you ask for, etc.?

Decide on a delegation leader or leaders. These will initiate the discussions and speak first in the negotiation sessions. The others will come in and provide support if necessary.

3 Now it's time for the negotiation to begin. The SELLERS and BUYERS meet. The aim is to come to a written agreement which you can each take back to your head office. The CONTROLLER will tell you how long you have to reach an agreement.

4 When the negotiation is over, all the sellers and the buyers should meet in separate areas and report back to each other on their results.

Sellers Tell the other group how satisfactory the first round has been. Announce how much you have sold and at what prices, etc. If no satisfactory result has been achieved, discuss what to do next.

Buyers Tell the other group how satisfactory the first round has been. Announce how much you have bought and at what prices, etc. If no satisfactory result has been achieved, discuss what to do next.

5 *Work in two groups or as a class* Finally, discuss these questions:

- How did you feel at each stage of the simulation?
- What did you learn from doing this simulation?
- If you could do the whole simulation again, what would you do differently?

"We've tried everything: refinancing, cutting costs, parties, clowns, trained seals ..."

15 A special project

JANUARY: The product

Your firm produces a range of delicious, high-quality main courses and desserts that are a speciality of your region. They are sold in supermarkets and to the catering trade. The products are ready to cook in a microwave or conventional oven.

1 *Work in small groups* Design your own new product. This will be a range of fresh, ready-to-cook specialities of *your* region or country. Think of a good brand name.

2 Give a presentation, describing your product to the other groups.

3 Decide which of the products will be most likely to succeed in the British and American markets. From now on *this* will be the product you're going to manufacture and market.

Telford. World class companies in a world class location.

Over 1000 companies, including 140 from overseas, have relocated to Telford (so you wouldn't be the first to put a toe in the water).

Telford.
development agency

. . . 9.5 million potential customers right on the doorstep and with 2 free ports and air freight facilities only 40 minutes away – international markets are within easy reach . . .

. . . Commercial property and development land at competitive prices, with grants available for construction, refurbishment, research and development and marketing . . .

. . . The advice and expertise offered by the local authority is second to none – making relocation painless . . .

. . . The choice, size and style of housing is wide with prices well below the national average.

METROPOLITAN
WIGAN
The Formula For Success.

Get the facts from Richard Jones,
Economic Development Unit,
(Dept. RU 1.10) P.O. Box 36,
Wigan Metropolitan Borough Council,
New Town Hall, Library Street,
Wigan, WN1 1NN.
Telephone (0942) 827729.

Photographed at the award winning
Kilhey Court, Wigan. Ideal venue for business
lunches, conferences and functions.

FEBRUARY: Finding a location

In March SPECIAL PROJECT TEAMS will be responsible for choosing a new location where the product will be manufactured and marketed in the UK and the USA: one team in the UK and one team in the USA. When the factory comes on line, the team will manage it during the first couple of years.

1 Decide on your criteria for choosing a location by grading these points in order of importance:

low cost of premises
availability of supplies
good, cheap housing
language
nearby airport
city or country

low taxes for new businesses
good road communications
closeness to principal markets
availability of cheap skilled workers
quality of life: convenience, facilities, etc.
development area or large city

What other factors are important, do you think?

2 Look at these maps of possible sites: which seem to be more suitable, according to the criteria you've just established?

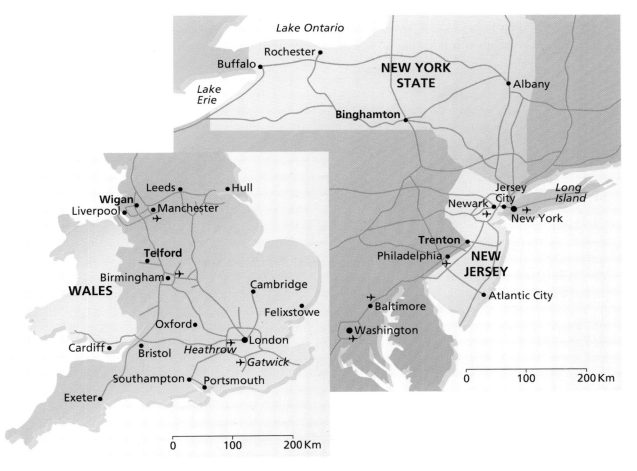

3 The CONTROLLER will tell you which team you're in and which country you're being sent to.

Finally, the CONTROLLER will hand out the documents you'll need for March. Read these through before the next lesson.

MARCH: Choosing the location and the personnel

Work in your team during the first five steps

1 First of all, read this memo from the Board:

> **TO:** Special project teams
> **FROM:** Board of Directors
>
> · Both plants will be semi-automated. Provisional orders have been placed for the special ovens and packaging machines.
> · There will be approximately 50 production staff in each plant at start-up, rising to 100 in 2—3 years.
> · Plant and offices will be on the same site. Marketing, sales and production will be working in close co-operation to adapt the product to local customers' requirements: supermarket chains may require 'own label' brands, ingredients may have to be changed to suit local tastes, etc.
> · Available buildings will be used.

2 Now that you've studied the documents about the various sites, find out what your colleagues' impressions and reactions are.

3 ◎◎ You'll hear a report from a colleague of yours who has visited the sites. Make notes on the most interesting points they make about each location.

4 Decide on the best location for your premises. Remember that you'll be living there yourself for a year or longer!

At least twice during March, one of you should phone one of your counterparts in the other country and find out what they have decided so far. Make notes during the call and then tell the other members of your team what you've found out.

5 Draft a brief outline explaining how you'll run your department to make sure your staff work happily and efficiently.

FAX a copy of this to your counterparts in the other country.

The members of your team will fill many of the top managerial positions:
- What posts will you each take?
- What specialists will you need to recruit locally for your management team?

6 Finally, both teams should meet to exchange experiences and discuss what has been done this month.

7 The CONTROLLER will give you the documents you'll need for April. Read these through before the next lesson.

APRIL: Suppliers & distribution / Marketing & sales

This month, the members of each team are divided into two groups. Each group will have to deal with a different part of the project. One group in each team will be discussing MATERIALS, SUPPLIES AND DISTRIBUTION, the other MARKETING AND SALES.

1 All the information you need for this month can be found in the document you have been given.

At least twice during April, one of you should phone one of your counterparts in the other country and get a progress report from them. Make notes during the call and then tell the other members of your group what you've found out.

2 Towards the end of the month, rejoin the other members of your own team and hold an informal meeting to find out what they have been doing this month.

MAY: The meeting

By now, both teams' final plans have been submitted to the board of directors for approval.

1 The CONTROLLER will give each team a fax to read: find out your colleagues' reactions to the information it contains, and decide what action to take.

2 So, there's going to be a meeting. Prepare your team's contribution to the meeting. Each member of your team should speak about a different aspect of the project. Decide which member of your team you'd like to chair the meeting.

3 **THE MEETING** The final meeting is held, with both teams putting forward their arguments.

DE-BRIEFING: Follow-up discussion

Work as a whole class Discuss these questions about the simulation:

- What happened in your team?
- What difficulties did you encounter?
- What was the most difficult part of the simulation for you?
- If you could do the simulation over again, what would you do differently?
- In what ways are real-life situations similar to the events in the simulation?

"We've polluted the air and water. Now our employees won't live here, so we're moving our headquarters to another county."

Files

1 You are in the A Team.
Choose one of the surnames and positions below for this role-play activity. Use your OWN real first name and title (*Mr*, *Ms*, *Dr*, etc.).
Write your full name and position on a badge or label, so that everyone can see who you are.

SURNAMES:
Rossi   Mackenzie   Jabbari   Schmidt   Martin   da Silva   Gomez
Foster   Kobayashi   O'Neill   Lefèvre   Cartier   Bellini
– *or another surname*

POSITIONS:
managing director   training officer   production manager   vice-chairman
purchasing manager   personnel manager   export sales manager
chief designer   sales director   public relations officer   marketing director
vice-president
– *or another position*

Imagine that the members of your team all work for ACME Industries. You're going to meet some visitors (members of the B Team). Introduce them to your colleagues.

1 A visitor from the B Team will introduce him or herself to you. Talk to this person for a minute or so.

2 Find a colleague to introduce your visitor to. At the same time you will be introduced to another visitor. Say goodbye to your first visitor and then start a conversation with the second visitor. Talk to this person for a minute or so.

3 Repeat step **2** with a different colleague.

4 Continue until your teacher asks you to stop.

5 Look at File **31** and choose a new identity. Play the role of a visitor this time.

---

2 Dictate these names and addresses to your partner:

Dr Hamish MacPherson
Rannoch Enterprises p.l.c.
45–55 Queen Street
Glasgow
GL1 8PG
SCOTLAND

Señora Maria Castillo Gomez
Ecuador Internacional SA
Calle Naranjo 50
46011 Valencia
SPAIN

Mr Hidetoshi Mayagi
Crown Products Ltd
40–5 Chajiri-cho
Arashiyama
Nishikyo
Kyoto-shi
JAPAN

3 You work for Utopia Products. You'll have to make two calls to Europrint and reply to two calls from them. To design the packaging and the labels, they need to have an actual prototype of your product, not just a specification.

① Make the 1st call:

A prototype of your product is now ready – offer to send one to Europrint.

Wait for a reply and then say goodbye.

② Then wait for the 2nd call …
Your reply to the 2nd call:

No, all the printing must be done by yourselves.

③ Make the 3rd call:

Request a quote for 5,000 items instead of the 3,500 previously quoted.

④ Your reply to the 4th call:

Agree to two deliveries – or insist on a single delivery (if you prefer).

---

4 Use your own name. You work for a subsidiary of Medusa S.A.
Call your firm's head office and find out the name, address and phone number of *Mr or Mrs G. Peters*, who lives somewhere in Switzerland.
You haven't spoken before to the person you're calling.

➡ When the call is finished, look at File **5**.

---

5 Use your own name. You are still working for a subsidiary of Medusa S.A. You'll receive a call. The information that the caller requires may be given in either of these files:

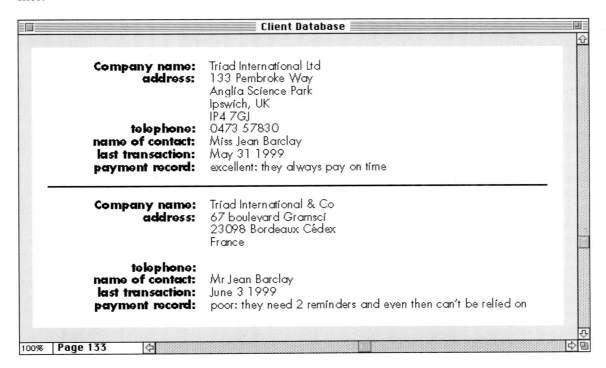

```
┌──────────────────────────── Client Database ════════════════════════════┐
│                                                                          │
│     Company name:   Triad International Ltd                              │
│          address:   133 Pembroke Way                                     │
│                     Anglia Science Park                                  │
│                     Ipswich, UK                                          │
│                     IP4 7GJ                                              │
│         telephone:  0473 57830                                           │
│   name of contact:  Miss Jean Barclay                                    │
│   last transaction: May 31 1999                                          │
│    payment record:  excellent: they always pay on time                   │
│  ──────────────────────────────────────────────────────                 │
│     Company name:   Triad International & Co                             │
│          address:   67 boulevard Gramsci                                 │
│                     23098 Bordeaux Cédex                                 │
│                     France                                               │
│         telephone:                                                       │
│   name of contact:  Mr Jean Barclay                                      │
│   last transaction: June 3 1999                                          │
│    payment record:  poor: they need 2 reminders and even then can't be relied on │
│                                                                          │
│ 100%  Page 133                                                           │
└──────────────────────────────────────────────────────────────────────────┘
```

6 You are the caller, Mr/Ms Tanaka.

- You met Mr/Ms Suarez at a trade fair last year. He/she may be interested in placing an order for some of your products.
- Call him/her and invite him/her to be your guest for lunch next Thursday when you'll be in town.
- Ask him/her to suggest a nice restaurant near his/her office.
- Find out what sort of restaurant it is and how you can get there on foot from the central rail station.
- Ask what time you should book a table.

When the call is over, the 'Observer(s)' will give you feedback on your performance.
Then, if you're in a group of three, look at File **7** for the next role-play.
(In a group of four, look at File **38**.)

---

7 You are Mr/Ms Peterson, in charge of shipping customers' orders and answering queries about delayed shipments.

These orders have been held up for the reasons given:
- ARG 4581 – delay due to rejection by Quality Control.
  Revised shipment date: 30th of this month.
- RAJ 4581 – delay due to staff sickness in Production Dept.
  Revised shipment date some time next week. Air freight at no extra charge.

When the call is over, the 'Observer(s)' will give you feedback on your performance.
Then look at File **8** for the next role-play.

---

8 You are an 'Observer'.

① Before the call begins look at your partners' instructions in Files **40** and **66**.

② Listen to your partners on the phone and make notes on their performance, according to the Observer's guidelines on page 32.

③ Give them feedback on their performance.

④ If you are in a group of three, look at File **10** for the last stage of this role-play.
(In a group of four, student A looks at File **41** while D looks at File **10**.)

9 You work in the Publicity Office of a company.

1 You start the conversation. Explain that a visitor is expected and ask whether your colleague in the design department will be available to meet her.
2 The visitor will be in the city from 14th–18th November. Any morning from 11.30 onwards and the afternoon of 15th November.
3 Ask if that is the only free occasion. And ask your colleague to make a note in his/her diary.

---

10 You are the caller, Mr/Ms Robinson.

- Call the Hotel Cambridge to confirm your reservations for tomorrow night for three nights: one double and one single room.
- The person staying in the single room (Mr Greenwood) will require the room for an extra night – is this OK?
- You will be arriving at 11 pm, so make sure the rooms are kept for you till then. You will be paying by Diner's Club card (#777 4580 2132 9).
- Will you be able to get a meal in the hotel when you arrive?

When the call is over, the 'Observer(s)' will give you feedback on your performance.

… You have now reached the end of this activity.

---

11 This diagram shows the structure of a company. Your partner has the missing information.

Ask questions like these about the company's structure to find the information you require:

Who is in charge of . . . ?   *Who reports to . . . ?*
Who reports to the . . . ?   *What does . . . do?*

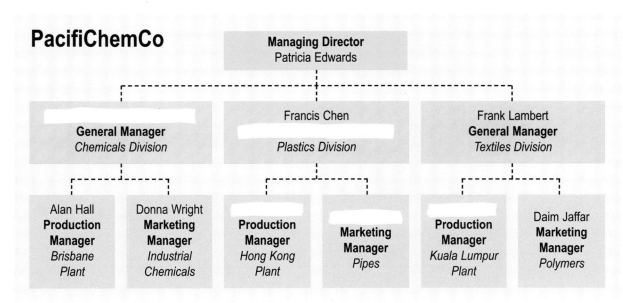

12 Your partner at the other end of the phone line has another copy of this price list. Find the missing information by asking questions like these:

> *Could you tell me how much item number 4478A costs in dollars?*
> *Do you know what the dimensions of item 4483 are?*

Code no.	Description	Prices in $ & £		Delivery
4478	green 58 x 72 cm PVC		£25.75	3 weeks
4478A	white 58 x 72 cm PVC		£24.85	5 weeks
4479	pink 44 x 72 cm heavy paper		£16.75	immediate
4480	red 88 x 88 cm PVC		£60.75	10 days
4482	blue 12 x 65 cm polystyrene		£9.75	4 weeks
4483	black ⬛ cm PVC	*discontinued: not available*		
4487	green ⬛ cm nylon	$15.00	£11.50	
4487B	white ⬛ cm nylon	$14.00	£11.00	
4488	clear ⬛ cm PVC	$89.50	£68.25	only

---

13 You are Jim Dale, Sales Director of Dale & Sons Batteries, Manchester. You are about to announce a new lightweight zinc cadmium battery, the DALE HERCULES, especially designed for electric vehicles.

Read this information before the call starts:

- Say that you know Broadway's requirements and your new Hercules is ideal for them.
- Prototypes are available now for testing.
- You are now tooling up for production to begin next week.
- Quote a firm shipping date of 4 weeks from today (5 November).
- Say that you can deliver for 10% less than Arcolite's price.

---

14 You are the proprietor of Agencia Léon of Mexico City. Make sure AntiSpy answers these questions:

- Are batteries rechargeable on 220 & 110 volt and both 50 & 60 cycles (Hz)?
- Will it operate directly from mains if batteries are low?
- Can it interfere with other phones in same building?
- Ask for DDP price for 10 to be shipped immediately.

➡ When you've finished, look at File **15**.

---

15 You work in the Export Sales Department of AntiSpy Products. Answer the phone and give the caller any information he or she requires. Consult your printout in ❹❸ on page 60.

16 This fax arrived on 18 July:

From Naves Limón

Thanks for your quotation no 0067. We wish to order two PB 5000 at your quoted total CIF price of one hundred and eighty seven thousand, eight hundred and fifty dollars including special anchors.

One customer who is waiting has already paid us a deposit. Please ship as soon as possible. Confirm definite delivery date to Puerto Limón. Please confirm 12 month warranty, replacement parts by air freight, as promised by Mr Richardson. Awaiting your reply.

Best,

Naves Limón

17 Look at this air waybill. In your copy all the figures in the gross weights (in kilos-K) column and some of the chargeable weights are missing. Ask your partner to dictate the missing figures to you.

When you have finished, check you have noted the correct figures. If you have time, as a final check write out the figures in words as you would say them.

No. of Pieces RCP	Gross Weight	kg lb	Rate Class	Commodity Item No.	Chargeable Weight	Rate Charge	Total	Nature and Quantity of Goods (incl. Dimensions or Volume)
1		K	N		15.5	2.050	31.775	Plugs
1		K	N			2.050	48.175	Plugs
1		K	N		21.0	2.050	43.050	Electrical sockets
1		K	N		19.5	2.050	39.975	Electrical sockets
3		K	C			1.050	0.525	Advertising displays
7							163.500	

Prepaid / Weight Charge / Collect / Other Charges

18 You are the assistant clerk at Finntec. These are the things you should refer to in your phone call to Mr Julio Martinez:

1 You call Julio Martinez. Enquire whether he has received the delivery note and invoice for the A6D sensor switches order.

2 Inform him that a revised price list now applies to the A6D sensor switches. Remind him that according to the quotation, the price list is subject to change. The invoice listing the new price of $1.80 was sent without noticing the discrepancy with the original quotation (at $1.60).

3 Normally Mr Julio Martinez pays his monthly account punctually, but you have not yet received payment for last month's account. Ask if there is some problem.

4 Apologize to Mr Julio Martinez for the delivery discrepancy. He is a long-standing customer, so you believe what he says. Ask for written confirmation of the delivery and billing discrepancy.

19 You are the credit controller. You begin by calling the customer. These are the points you should try to clarify:

1 You are waiting for a cheque to arrive. Find out the apparent reason for the non-payment.
2 Say you will keep calling until the cheque arrives.
3 Ask the customer for the date the cheque was sent, whether it went by normal mail or recorded delivery. Ask how much the cheque was for and what the cheque number was.
4 Try to extract a promise of payment by a specific date. Otherwise …

---

20 You and your partner are colleagues who work in the same office. Make the following complaints and apologies:

❶ Apologize because you have forgotten to phone Los Angeles. Now it's too late because it's after office hours for them.

❷ Complain because your colleague didn't check with you before placing the order with the people in Toronto.

❸ Apologize because you have left a file at home. It contains the documents your colleague needs to have for a meeting today.

❹ Apologize because you didn't send the quote to Garfield International yesterday. Now you may have lost the order.

❺ Complain because your colleague always gets back to the office late after lunch. You always have to answer the phone for him or her.

➡ Respond to your colleague's complaints and apologies.

---

21 You are calling to book three rooms at the Rio Othon Palace Hotel or the Caesar Park Hotel from 9 to 15 May.

BEFORE YOU START, look at the points below – make sure you cover all of them. Make notes during the call.

1 Introduce yourself (your name and company).
2 Find out if any rooms are available from 9 May to 15 May.
   Explain your requirements: the rooms are for yourself, Ms Castel and Mr & Mrs Holzger (who require twin beds).
3 Find out the cost of single and double rooms.
   Find out the difference between rooms at different prices.
   Find out whether the rates include breakfast.
4 Book two doubles at the lower price and one at the higher price.
5 Ask for quiet rooms – preferably with a view of the sea.
   Decide whether to have all three rooms with balcony + view.
6 Ask them to send you four copies of the hotel brochure.

22 Note from Mr Richardson:

> Please send a letter to Naves Limón in Costa Rica.
> Find out:
> – Are they satisfied with the order?
> – Can we provide any after-sales advice?
> Encourage repeat order.

---

23 Design a questionnaire to find out the importance of various factors in choosing a holiday destination.

Ask people to decide how important these factors are on a scale 1 to 10 (or 1 to 5 – if you prefer) for a main holiday and for a second holiday:

different way of life	night life	good food
historic places	beautiful scenery	meeting people
learn new things	bargain prices	gifts & souvenirs
summer sports	winter sports	relaxation
outdoor activities	visiting friends & relations	
part of longer trip	no language problems	

---

24 These are your department's suggestions. Add your own ideas.

> – more staff parties and picnics
> – better toilets and showers
> – open the roof garden to the staff
> – more comfortable tables and chairs in the staff canteen

---

25 The estimated costs of some of the proposals are:

> — Rebuilding toilets and showers: £6,500
> — New tables and chairs for canteen: £1,150
> — Safety work on roof garden: £1,950
> — Staff parties/picnics: minimal cost
>   to the company

26

1. Look at these diagrams. Work out together how to explain to another person – in your own words – how the product works.

2. When you're ready, split up and form a pair with one of the other members of the group. Explain your product to them, and find out from them how a hard disk works.

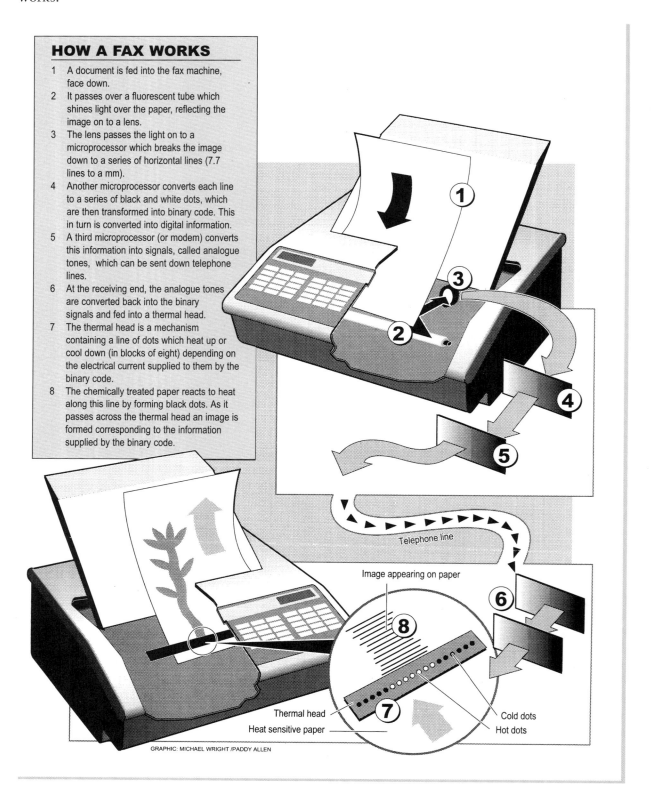

HOW A FAX WORKS

1. A document is fed into the fax machine, face down.
2. It passes over a fluorescent tube which shines light over the paper, reflecting the image on to a lens.
3. The lens passes the light on to a microprocessor which breaks the image down to a series of horizontal lines (7.7 lines to a mm).
4. Another microprocessor converts each line to a series of black and white dots, which are then transformed into binary code. This in turn is converted into digital information.
5. A third microprocessor (or modem) converts this information into signals, called analogue tones, which can be sent down telephone lines.
6. At the receiving end, the analogue tones are converted back into the binary signals and fed into a thermal head.
7. The thermal head is a mechanism containing a line of dots which heat up or cool down (in blocks of eight) depending on the electrical current supplied to them by the binary code.
8. The chemically treated paper reacts to heat along this line by forming black dots. As it passes across the thermal head an image is formed corresponding to the information supplied by the binary code.

Telephone line

Image appearing on paper

Thermal head
Heat sensitive paper

Cold dots
Hot dots

GRAPHIC: MICHAEL WRIGHT /PADDY ALLEN

154

27 You are the customer. You answer the phone.

1 Offer to chase up the account and see what has happened. Give plausible arguments for the delay.
2 Say that to the best of your knowledge the cheque has been posted.
3 Offer to send the information requested.
4 Offer to do your best to rectify the situation, if it is as stated.

---

28 You are area sales representative for an importer. The customer is chief buyer for a mail order company or chain store. You know this customer well. Give your customer this information:

- Each recorder is packed in protective foam inside a very attractive, illustrated carton (about half the size of this page).
- Batteries not supplied: they might leak.
- You could supply suitable batteries separately @ £58 per 100.
- You have stock for immediate delivery. Further shipments take four weeks.
- The wholesale price is £399 for a carton of 20 (retail price about £49.95).

TLC Tele Recorder

---

29 You are the buyer for your company. You are calling to negotiate an order.

1 State that you need 10,000 cartons of yogurt by three weeks today, at SFr (Swiss Francs) 1,500 per 100 cartons.
2 Make it clear that you want this for a customer, three weeks from today's date.
3 Ask how many cartons they can deliver for three weeks from now.
4 Suggest that you could go to another supplier, although you have been satisfied with this company in the past. But you could offer to take the order somewhere else.
5 Try to find out if the other side want to keep your order. (Because you know the alternative distributors are a little dearer.)
6 If no suggestion comes from the other side suggest that you are willing to compromise on the delivery time if the price is reduced.
7 Accept if the conditions are favourable, within 10% of your desired price SFr (Swiss Francs) 1,350.

30

You both work in the sales department of your company. You must agree and try to decide what terms, price, conditions, etc. you are prepared to sell the product at.

The product is an electrical component. These are the limits within which you can move:

1 What price you will accept: between $25 and $36
2 Quantities: can supply up to five hundred
3 Delivery date proposed: between six and 18 months from now
4 Specifications deliverable: they range from 250 to 270 rpm   [revolutions per minute]
5 Guarantee period offered: from six months to a year
6 Conditions of payment expected: ex-works, but will accept FOB
7 Limited target: would like to sell a sample plus firm order

Make notes of the terms and points agreed with your colleague before the 'real negotiation' with the buyer begins.

31

You are in the B Team.

Choose one of these surnames and nationalities for this role-play activity. Use your OWN first name and title (Mr, Ms, Dr, etc.).

Legrand	Geneva, Switzerland	Harris	Plymouth, England
Gabrielli	Milan, Italy	Müller	Munich, Germany
Yip	Singapore	Rockford	Detroit, USA
Beaumont	Lille, France	Martens	Brussels, Belgium
Vlachou	Salonika, Greece	Carreras	Barcelona, Spain
Oliveira	São Paulo, Brazil	Fukuda	Osaka, Japan
Wallnöfer	Vienna, Austria	McKinley	Edinburgh, Scotland

Imagine that each of you is a VISITOR to ACME Industries. You're each going to meet someone who works there (members of the A Team). They will introduce you to their colleagues.

1 Introduce yourself to someone who works at ACME Industries. Talk to this person for a minute or so.

2 Your host will introduce you to one of his or her colleagues. Say goodbye to your host and then talk to this new person for a minute or so.

3 Step 2 will be repeated with a different ACME employee.

4 Continue until your teacher asks you to stop.

5 Look at File 1 and choose a new identity. Play the role of a member of ACME Industries staff this time.

32

You are the seller.

You are trying to sell an electrical component.

You must remain within the limits you agreed with your partner in step D 1 on page 140. Consult your notes.

• Start the proposal phase of the negotiation.
• It is your task now to negotiate with the buyer and to reach a reasonable conclusion which both you and the buyer can be satisfied with.

33 Dictate these names and addresses to your partner:

Mr Hugh O'Shea
Gloucester Products Ltd
114 North Shields Road
Newcastle NE5 47G
ENGLAND

Mlle Annick Dubois
S.E.B.A.R.A.
123 rue de la Paix
5100 Reims
FRANCE

Mrs Leena Suominnen
Koivisto Kirja Kauppa OY
Kirkkokatu 28
20100 Turku
FINLAND

---

34 You work for Europrint. You'll have to reply to two calls from Utopia Products and make two calls to them. In order to design the packaging and labels, you need to have an actual prototype of their product, not just a specification.

1 Your reply to the 1st call:

Request Utopia send product prototype by courier right away.

Wait for a reaction to this and then say goodbye.

2 Then make the 2nd call:

Is it OK to sub-contract printing of the stick-on labels?

3 Your reply to the 3rd call:

Offer to get your local agent to discuss this.

4 Make the 4th call:

Is it OK to deliver order in two batches: first on 1st May, second on 1st June?

---

35 Use your own name. You work in the head office of Medusa S.A. The caller works in a subsidiary company, but you haven't been in touch before. The address the caller requires might be either of these:

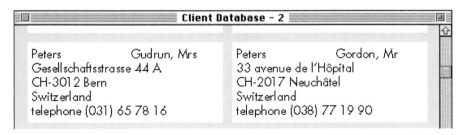

Peters Gudrun, Mrs	Peters Gordon, Mr
Gesellschaftsstrasse 44 A	33 avenue de l'Hôpital
CH-3012 Bern	CH-2017 Neuchâtel
Switzerland	Switzerland
telephone (031) 65 78 16	telephone (038) 77 19 90

➡ When the call is finished, look at File **36**.

36 You are still working in the head office of Medusa S.A. Use your own name. Call the person you spoke to before in the subsidiary company. You require some information about a company who are about to place an order. Make a note of all the details you need:

Company name: *Triad International*
address:

name of contact: *Mr (or Miss?) Jean Barclay*
last transaction: *last May or June*
payment record:

---

37 You are Mr/Ms Suarez, in charge of buying supplies for your firm.

- You met Mr/Ms Tanaka at a trade fair in his/her country last year. He/she supplies a product you may be interested in. You haven't heard from him/her since then.
- Next Thursday you are free for lunch but have to be back in the office at 2.30 for a meeting.
- If you are asked to recommend a restaurant, suggest a place you *really* do like in your own town.

When the call is over, the 'Observer(s)' will give you feedback on your performance.
Then look at File **38** for the next role-play.

---

38 You are an 'Observer'.

1 Before the call begins look at your partners' instructions in Files **65** and **7**.

2 Listen to your partners on the phone and make notes on their performance, according to the Observer's guidelines on page 32.

3 Give them feedback on their performance.

4 If you are in a group of three, look at File **40** for the next stage of this role-play. (In a group of four, student A looks at File **8** while B looks at File **40**.)

---

39 You work in the Design Office of a company.

1 Say you are willing to meet the visitor and show her the department. Ask when the visitor is expected.
2 Explain that you are very busy all that week. But you might be able to find half an hour for the morning of 15th November.
3 Reluctantly agree that you will be able to receive the guest, and offer to have lunch with her.

40 You are the caller, Mr/Ms Steiner of Avco International.

- Call the Provence Restaurant (the best in town) to book a private room for a visiting group of clients next Tuesday evening, ideally from 7.30.
- There will be 10 to 14 in your party. You won't know exactly how many until Tuesday morning.
- Three of your guests are vegetarians – does this present any problems?

When the call is over, the 'Observer(s)' will give you feedback on your performance.

Then, if you're in a group of three, look at File **41** for the next role-play. (In a group of four, look at File **49**.)

---

41 You are the reception manager at the Hotel Cambridge.

- Someone will call to confirm his/her reservations. The computer confirms that the caller has a firm reservation for a twin-bedded room and a single room from tomorrow for three nights.
- There is a trade fair this week and all your single rooms are fully booked for the next ten days. There are one or two doubles available.
- You will only hold reserved rooms till 9 pm unless you have confirmed reservations by American Express or Diner's Club.
- Note the caller's name and the name of the person who will occupy the single room. Also find out his/her contact phone number.
- The Coffee Shop serves meals till 2 am.

When the call is over, the 'Observer(s)' will give you feedback on your performance.

… You have now reached the end of this activity.

---

42 Call Agencia Léon in Mexico. Reassure them that you have consulted your technical department and they confirm that:

- Batteries are rechargeable on all voltages.
- A universal plug is fitted for mains operation and recharging.
- It can interfere with radio reception in the same room but not with any other phones.

Consult your printout in **A** **3** on page 60 to quote price and delivery.

➡ When you've finished, look at File **45**.

43 This diagram shows the structure of a company. Your partner has the missing information. Ask questions like these about the company's structure to find the information you require:

Who is in charge of ...?   Who reports to ...?   Who reports to the ...?   What does ... do?

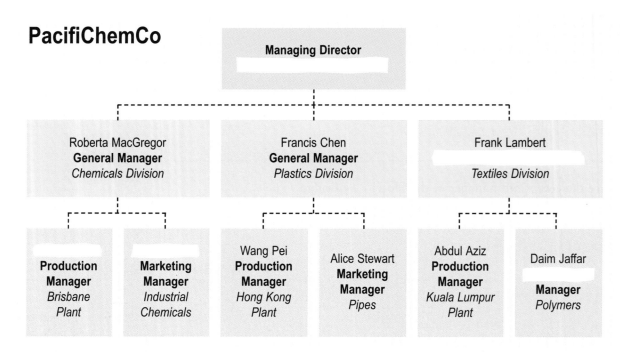

PacifiChemCo

Managing Director

Roberta MacGregor
General Manager
Chemicals Division

Francis Chen
General Manager
Plastics Division

Frank Lambert

Textiles Division

Production Manager
Brisbane Plant

Marketing Manager
Industrial Chemicals

Wang Pei
Production Manager
Hong Kong Plant

Alice Stewart
Marketing Manager
Pipes

Abdul Aziz
Production Manager
Kuala Lumpur Plant

Daim Jaffar

Manager
Polymers

---

44 Your partner at the other end of the phone line has another copy of this price list. Find the missing information by asking questions like these:

> *Could you tell me what the dimensions of item 4478A are?*
> *Do you know what the delivery is on item 4478?*

Code no.	Description	Prices in $ & £		Delivery
4478	green 58 ▮▮ cm PVC	$33.85	£25.75	▮ weeks
4478A	whit▮ ▮▮ PVC	$32.65	£24.85	▮▮ks
4479	pink ▮▮ ▮eavy paper	$22.00	£16.75	▮▮diate
4480	red 8▮ ▮C	$79.75	£60.75	10 days
4482	blue 12▮ ▮▮ cm polystyrene	$12.60	£9.75	4 weeks
4483	black 43 x 17 cm PVC	▮▮ued: not available		
4487	green 44.5 x 25 cm nylon		▮1.50	7 days
4487B	white 44.5 x 25 cm nylon		▮1.00	14 days
4488	clear 78 x 95 cm PVC	$▮▮	£68.25	to order only

45 You work for Agencia Léon. You are interested in the GR440 Screen Spy product that AntiSpy manufactures. Call AntiSpy to make enquiries about the product:

- *Find out how much it costs and how quickly you can get one delivered.*
- *Say that you are prepared to pay a cash deposit.*
- *You can collect it yourself from their warehouse in California.*
- *There is no problem with getting an import licence.*

46 These faxes arrived on 19 July:

From Alpha Marine

The goods you require are now available from stock. We will deliver in our own transport on 19 August. Please advise if goods required more urgently. You could arrange collection ex-works by your own carrier if desired.
Regards.

From Lysander Freight and Shipping

We have arranged for two forty-foot open top containers to be delivered to your factory to arrive at 9 am on 16 August. They will be collected for onward shipment to docks on 23 August in time for booked passage on 30 August on m/v Caribbean Star to Puerto Limón. Arriving Puerto Limón 10 or 11 September.
Please confirm that this arrangement is agreeable.
Best regards.

47 Look at this air waybill. In your copy all the figures in the totals column are missing and also some of the charges. Ask your partner to dictate the missing figures to you.

When you have finished, check you have noted the correct figures. If you have time, as a final check write out the figures in words as you would say them.

Handling Information	AIKASHINKO AWB 121-18107600 OSAKA via NARITA					Keep packets dry. Kaiji Kentei Kyokai 2-Chome, Hanamitsu-cho Kobe, Japan		Notify:	
No. of Pieces RCP	Gross Weight	kg lb	Rate Class	Commodity Item No.	Chargeable Weight	Rate / Charge	Total	Nature and Quantity of Goods (incl. Dimensions or Volume)
1	15.5	K	N		15.5	2.050		Plugs
1	23.2	K	N		23.5	-		Plugs
1	20.8	K	N		21.0	2.050		Electrical sockets
1	19.5	K	N		19.5	2.050		Electrical sockets
3	0.2	K	C		0.5			Advertising displays
7	79.2							

Prepaid /	Weight Charge /	Collect /	Other Charges

48 You are Julio Martinez, chief clerk for Frigorifico Ameglio S.A. You answer a call from the assistant clerk of Finntec. Respond to what he or she tells you and then mention the following points:

1 *Reply that you do not have a record of the delivery of the items and the invoice in front of you at the moment. Ask what the problem is.*

2 *Your company is aware that the original order was based on the quotation of $1.60. Thank them for the information about the new price.*

3 *Explain that you have only just returned from a holiday. You now have the file in front of you. Explain that your payment clerk noted on the delivery note that you only received 25 gross. Moreover, it appears as if the invoice was automatically paid by the Accounts Department minus the amount for 10 gross at the old price.*

4 *Offer to pay the difference or to add it to the next order.*

---

49 You are an 'Observer'.

❶ Before the call begins look at your partners' instructions in Files **10** and **41**.

❷ Listen to your partners on the phone and make notes on their performance, according to the Observer's guidelines on page 32.

❸ Give them feedback on their performance.

… You have now reached the end of this activity.

---

50 You are the Reservations Manager at the Rio Othon Palace Hotel or Caesar Park Hotel. BEFORE YOU START, look at the points below – make sure you cover all of them. Make notes during the call.

1 Answer the phone, say hello and introduce yourself (name of hotel, your name and function). Ask how you can help.
Note down the caller's name and use the name during the call.

2 Check if the last date is the leaving date or 'night of' date.
Find out what rooms the caller requires.
For the week they require you have only one single available. A single is much smaller than a double. Doubles for single occupancy would be more comfortable.

3 Quote your rates per night:
RIO OTHON PALACE: $165 single; $200 or $290 double
CAESAR PARK: $130 single; $170 or $230 double
The top price rooms have a balcony and sea view. All rooms have bath and shower, colour TV, telephone, minibar, air conditioning.
Confirm that the rooms requested are available.
The room rate includes buffet breakfast, the rate is per room (not per person).

4 Ask for the caller's name, address and contact phone number and fax number.
Ask for written confirmation by fax or letter, stating time of arrival.

5 Explain that all your rooms are quiet.
Explain that only rooms with a balcony have a view of the sea.

6 Read out your notes to make sure you have understood the details correctly.

51 You and your partner are colleagues who work in the same office. Make the following complaints and apologies:

1 Apologize because you've forgotten to get last year's sales figures from the Sales Manager. Now she has left the building.

2 Complain because your colleague made a long-distance private call on the office phone.

3 Complain because your colleague should have faxed New Orleans, not written a letter. A fax is quicker and more reliable than airmail.

4 Apologize because you have made an appointment for your colleague to see the Managing Director in five minutes' time – it was the only time the MD was free this week.

5 Complain because your colleague didn't contact the Computer Manager before sending in an order for some computer software.

➡ Respond to your colleague's complaints and apologies.

---

52 This fax arrived on 23 December from Costa Rica:

```
From Naves Limón

Merry Christmas! We are pleased to tell you that both vessels
have been delivered to our customers who are well pleased. We
have had several enquiries from other people in Costa Rica and
elsewhere in Central America. You can expect another order
from us in the New Year.
Would you consider us as your exclusive distributor in Central
America (not including Mexico or Panama)?
We look forward to hearing from you.
```

---

53 Make a list of five or more regions or countries that are in competition with yours. Design a questionnaire to find out people's attitudes to the less attractive features of these regions – and your own region.

Ask people which of these phrases describe each destination:

```
bad weather                  too far away
too expensive                unfriendly, gloomy people
hard to reach                language problems
nothing for children to do   no package tours available
too crowded                  no beaches
too quiet                    bad food
other (please specify):
```

54 These are your department's suggestions. Add your own ideas.

more flowers and plants in the offices
more flexibility about taking time off
better lighting and heating
more pictures and posters on the walls

---

55 The estimated costs of some of the proposals are:

— Replacing typing chairs £105; armchairs £155
— New coffee machine: £37 per week rental
— Crockery for canteen (with company logo): £350
— Extension to car park: £5,500

---

56 ❶ Look at these diagrams. Work out together how to explain to another person – in your own words – how the product works.

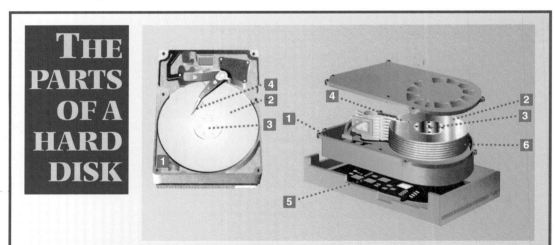

THE PARTS OF A HARD DISK

- The main assembly of the head-disk (1) holds the platters or disks (2).
- The platters or disks (2) store the data in concentric circles, known as tracks.
- At the centre is a spindle motor (3) which rotates the platters (2) at very precise speeds.
- While the platters are rotating, read/write heads (4) take data from and to tracks.
- A SCSI controller card (5) controls all the mechanical parts of the hard disk activity.
- In larger capacity drives there many platters and head assemblies that greatly improve the speed of the multiple activities (6).

A. Throughput

The amount of data that actually gets written or read in a given period of time is called the throughput.

B. Access time

Computers read and write data in very small amounts. They then have to prepare these clusters of data prior to writing them to disk or processing them once they have been read from disk. Every one of these read or write operations has a small amount of processing time involved which has to be added to the access time.

❷ When you're ready, split up and form a pair with one of the other members of the group. Explain your product to them, and find out from them how a fax machine works.

57 These are the correct names and addresses for exercise **2.2B**.

Mr George James
Managing Director
Alan and James Ltd
Quality House
77-81 London Road
Bristol
BL5 9AR
GREAT BRITAIN

Ms Alison Freeman
Marketing Co-ordinator
United Packaging Inc.
11 East Shore Drive
Green Bay
Wisconsin
WI 53405
USA

Mr R.G. Flinders
Sales Manager
Independent Products Pty
18 Canberra Way
Liverpool
NSW 2170
AUSTRALIA

Miss J.V. Bernstein
Candex Convention Organizer
Dominion Centre
80 Prince of Wales Drive
Ottawa
Ontario
KT5 1AQ
CANADA

---

58 You are area sales representative for an importer. The customer is chief buyer for a mail order company or chain store. You know this customer well. Give your customer this information:

- The alarm is in white.
- Batteries are not required, as it connects with the mains supply.
- Each alarm is packed in a sturdy brown cardboard box.
- The product is ready to use.
- You will have stock in two weeks.
- The wholesale price of the product is £400 for a carton of 20 (£44.95 retail).

---

59 You are in the sales department of your company. You'll receive a call from a buyer.

1 Reply that the largest quantity you can provide is 5,000 cartons, at SFr (Swiss Francs) 1,545 per 100 cartons.
2 State that you cannot deliver by three weeks from now.
3 State that for such large quantities the lead time is going to have to be much longer.
4 Suggest that you want to keep the order but know that you can only deliver 2,000 of the 5,000 cartons in three weeks.
5 Try to find out what the other side are prepared to do. Perhaps you can play for time, because you guess that the buyer will be eager to strike a deal ...
6 You guess that the buyer will be a good customer in years to come. So propose that you are prepared to come down in the price ...
7 Agree to the deal as long as the price does not fall below your accepted internal bottom limit, which is SFr (Swiss Francs) 1,468 per 100.

60

You both work in the buying department of your company. You must agree and try to decide what terms, price, conditions, etc. you are prepared to buy the product at.

The product is an electrical component. These are the limits within which you can move:

> 1 What price you will pay: from $23 to $34
> 2 Quantities: can eventually use five hundred, but only if satisfied with sample
> 3 Delivery date required: between six weeks and 13 months from now
> 4 Specifications really needed: they range from 280 to 300 rpm   [revolutions per minute]
> 5 Guarantee period requested: from a year to 18 months
> 6 Conditions of payment expected: CIF, but would settle for FOB
> 7 Limited target: would like to buy only one, plus firm order for 500 later, if satisfied

Make notes of the terms and points agreed with your colleague before the 'real negotiation' with the seller begins.

61

You are the buyer.

You are interested in buying an electrical component.

You must remain within the limits you agreed with your partner in step ❶❶ on page 140.

Consult your notes.

- Respond to the seller's first point.
- It is your task now to negotiate with the seller and to reach a reasonable conclusion which both you and the seller can be satisfied with.

62

Explain to your partner where to draw a CONTINUOUS LINE to create this picture:

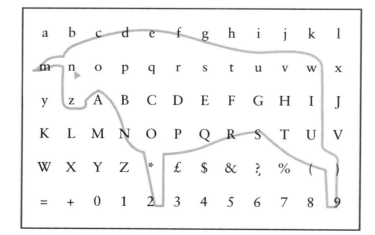

The line must go …

around   between   past   across   above   below   to the left of   to the right of

… the letters and numbers.

63 This is an improved version of the memo in **2.5🅐**.

MEMORANDUM

• •

TO: All members of staff, Northern Branch

FROM: KLJ

DATE: 2 December 1999

SUBJECT: LAPTOP COMPUTERS

The board urgently requires feedback on our experience with laptops in Northern Branch. I need to know, for my report:

1 What you personally use your laptop for and your reasons for doing this. If you are doing work that was formerly done by other staff, please justify this.
2 What software you use. Please name the applications and version numbers.
3 How many hours per day you spend actually using it.
4 How your laptop has not come up to your expectations.
5 What unanticipated uses you have found for your laptop, that others may want to share.

Please FAX this information directly to me by 5 pm on WEDNESDAY 7 December.

If you have any queries, please contact my assistant, Jane Simmonds, who will be visiting you on Tuesday 6 December.

Thank you for your help.

KLJ

---

64 You are an 'Observer'.

❶ Before the call begins look at your partners' instructions in Files **6** and **37**.

❷ Listen to your partners on the phone and make notes on their performance, according to the Observer's guidelines on page 32.

❸ Give them feedback on their performance.

❹ If you are in a group of three, look at File **65** for the next stage of this role-play. (In a group of four, student C looks at File **65** while D looks at File **7**.)

---

65 You are Mr/Ms LaRue, a customer. You are the caller.

- Call Mr/Ms Peterson to find out whether the goods you have ordered have been dispatched yet.
- The order number was RAJ 4581. The date you placed the order was January 16. If they haven't been sent, try to get him/her to hurry them up.
- Ask *exactly* when you can expect the goods to arrive. If necessary, he/she can call you back with this information (023 1550 extension 018).

When the call is over, the 'Observer(s)' will give you feedback on your performance.

Then look at File **66** for the next role-play.

66 You are the manager of the Provence Restaurant (the best in town). Your menu includes fresh fish and vegetarian dishes.

> - Accept a booking for your private room for next Tuesday. You require a written confirmation of this by letter or fax (015 458).
> - As you already have another party arriving at 7.30, any further parties should arrive at 8 for 8.30.
> - You need to know the *exact* number of places first thing on Tuesday (your early morning phone number is 015 454).

When the call is over, the 'Observer(s)' will give you feedback on your performance.

Look at File **49** for the last stage of this role-play.

---

67 This is a model version of the health and safety report on page 35:

To: Ms Renoir, Managing Director

From: (your name) **Date:**

<u>Office health and safety provisions</u>

As requested by the Managing Director on 30 March 1999, I have investigated the problems which have been raised concerning office health and safety.

  A study was made of all job-related illnesses during the past year. For example, it was found that a number of cases of symptoms of Repetitive Strain Injury (RSI) had been reported by the company physiotherapist. Meetings were held with union representatives and office managers to discuss what could be done.

<u>Proposals</u>

1 The safety regulations should be clearly displayed in the company's canteen and main offices.
2 Newly appointed staff should be made aware of the company's safety regulations and policy. In particular, they should be advised to take frequent breaks from the screen.
3 It is necessary to teach office staff how to position themselves, their chairs, desks and equipment.
4 It should be the responsibility of the departmental committee on health and safety to instruct new staff on procedures for handling office equipment and for securing electronic and mechanical machinery.
5 It was further noted that ventilation and air-filtering systems in offices require regular maintenance.
6 The union suggested that sub-standard furniture and equipment should be replaced. In particular:
   a) old-fashioned screens should be replaced — they are known to cause eyesight problems.
   b) office lighting should be carefully checked. Staff have complained of headaches after work; lighting is a large part of the problem. An important point to emphasize is that bright lights should not reflect on the screen.
   c) chairs with full back supports are essential. Many staff have complained of backache.

68 Explain to your partner where to draw a CONTINUOUS LINE to create this picture:

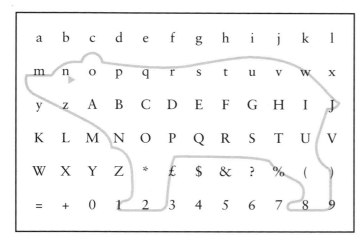

The line must go …
around   between   past   across   above   below   to the left of   to the right of
                                              … the letters and numbers.

---

69 This is an improved version of the Managing Director's memo on page 36:

Memorandum

FROM: The Managing Director	for	please
TO: Personnel Managers	ACTION	DISPLAY
	COMMENT	FILE
DATE: 27 April 1999	INFORMATION	RETURN
	DISCUSSION	PASS TO:

....

SUBJECT: Installation of clocking-in machines

The Board is thinking of installing an automatic
clocking-in system in the offices of each division. Before we
do this we need to know:

1 How the arrangements concerning breaks, especially lunch
  breaks, have been working.
2 How many machines we would need.
3 Whether time now lost through bad time-keeping would be
  saved.

Can you provide us with your views on:
- how the staff will react to the idea
- how we can deal with the union on the matter

If possible, I would like to receive your report before the
next Board Meeting on 1 June.

71 This fax arrived on 13 September:

```
FROM NAVES LIMÓN
We acknowledge safe arrival of two containers, now unpacked.
Both vessels are in perfect condition.
Thank you for your speedy and friendly service.
Please note: we asked for six copies of handbook for each vessel, not
six altogether. Please send further six copies by fastest route.
Best.
```

72 This is the fax you receive from Mr Julio Martinez:

FROM: JULIO MARTINEZ

Frigorifico Ameglio S.A.   **Colonia 1023**   **Montevideo**   **Uruguay**
Tel: (598) 2 21 08 24
FAX: +598 2 32 45 67

For the Attn of G. Aaltio   28 April 1999

Please send acknowledgement of receipt of payment for order No: 03764 soonest.

Regards

Julio Martinez

Julio Martinez

---

73 Most credits are fairly similar in appearance and contain the following details (numbers correspond to those in the example):

1 The name and address of the exporter
2 The expiry date
3 Precise instructions as to the documents against which payment is to be made
4 The terms of contract and shipment (i.e. whether 'EXW', 'FOB', 'CIF' etc.)
5 The type of credit (revocable or irrevocable)
6 The amount of the credit, in sterling or a foreign currency
7 The name and address of the importer
8 The name of the party on whom the bills of exchange are to be drawn, and whether they are to be at sight or of a particular tenor
9 A brief description of the goods covered by the credit
10 Whether the credit is available for one or several partshipments
11 Shipping details, including whether partshipments and/or transhipments are allowed. Also recorded should be the latest date for shipment and the names of the ports of shipment and discharge. (It may be in the best interest of the exporter for shipment to be allowed 'from any UK port' so that a choice is available if, for example, some ports are affected by strikes. The same applies for the port of discharge.)

74

                                                   13 August 1999

Dear Ms Santinelli,

Please find enclosed the outstanding cheque for SFr 19,564.00 (nineteen thousand five hundred and sixty-four Swiss francs).

We would like to thank you for your sympathetic and understanding actions. We shall do everything in our power to settle our accounts as promptly as possible in future.

Yours sincerely,

Wilhelm Becker

(Chief clerk, Accounts)

75　This fax has arrived from Uniplex srl in Pisa:

```
    Thank you very much for the order for 45 (forty-five) x 100
metre reels of 40 (forty) millimetre MCL88 cable.
    I confirm that this is available ex-stock and that we can ship
this at the end of this month. We shall begin packing tomorrow.
    I am confident that you will be impressed with the quality of
this product. We are pleased to be doing business with you and
look forward to continuing co-operation in the future.
    Our proforma invoice follows by airmail.
    Best wishes,
    Piero Conti, Export Manager, Uniplex Pisa
```

These are your records on the computer about the two firms:

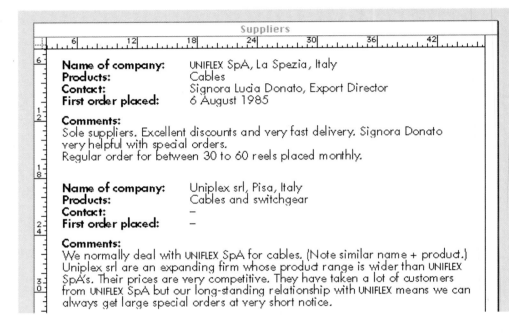

Suppliers

Name of company: UNIFLEX SpA, La Spezia, Italy
Products: Cables
Contact: Signora Lucia Donato, Export Director
First order placed: 6 August 1985

Comments:
Sole suppliers. Excellent discounts and very fast delivery. Signora Donato very helpful with special orders.
Regular order for between 30 to 60 reels placed monthly.

Name of company: Uniplex srl, Pisa, Italy
Products: Cables and switchgear
Contact: –
First order placed: –

Comments:
We normally deal with UNIFLEX SpA for cables. (Note similar name + product.) Uniplex srl are an expanding firm whose product range is wider than UNIFLEX SpA's. Their prices are very competitive. They have taken a lot of customers from UNIFLEX SpA but our long-standing relationship with UNIFLEX means we can always get large special orders at very short notice.

76　This fax has just arrived from Mr Reynard:

```
    Thank you for your letter of May 20. I was very sorry to hear about
your problems with our service agents. I had no idea that you were in
any way dissatisfied.
    If you had let me know earlier, I could have investigated this
immediately. Our service agents in your country are normally most
reliable and I can only assume that the particular engineer
responsible for your area is at fault.
    Let me assure you that our after-sales service to you in future
will be excellent. In future you will receive attention within 24
hours of calling the engineer.
    If you experience any other difficulties, please call me or fax me
at once and I will take immediate action.
    Again, let me say how sorry I am. When I have investigated the
causes of your difficulties, I will let you know the outcome.
    Best wishes,
```

Henry Reynard

➡ Draft another letter or fax – or make notes for a phone call to Mr Reynard.

77 Make a list of five or more regions or countries that are in competition with yours. Design a questionnaire to find out about people's attitudes to your region and to its competitors.

Ask people to rate each destination for its qualities on a scale 1 to 10 (or 1 to 5 – if you prefer):

```
good value for money    easy to get to      good facilities
good entertainment      health and sport    peace and quiet
friendliness            hospitality         wilderness
culture                 beautiful scenery   uniqueness
```

➡ And also ask them to describe each place in one sentence like this:

'*When I think of ___, I think of ___.*'

(e.g. '*When I think of Ruritania, I think of cold winds and a flat landscape.*')

---

78 These are your department's suggestions. Add your own ideas.

more comfortable chairs
a better coffee machine
real crockery and cutlery in the canteen instead of plastic
more car parking spaces

---

79 The estimated costs of some of the proposals are:

```
– Plants: £295 per floor + £55 monthly service
– One extra day unpaid leave: £520 in labour costs
– New lighting and heating system: £1,950 per floor
– Paintings: £7,000; framed posters: £550
```

---

80 You are going to chair the meeting.

Here are some tips for chairing a meeting:

1 Begin by stating the purpose of the meeting.
2 Give the name of the person you want to speak next.
3 Make sure everyone has a chance to give their views.
4 If someone is taking too long, say *Thank you* and name the next person who wants to speak.
5 If there is disagreement on any point, call for a vote.
6 Make sure one member of the group is keeping minutes: ask them to read out the notes at the end, if there's time.
7 Keep to the time limit: if necessary stop the discussion and summarize the conclusions and decisions you have come to.

81 This is a model application letter for the Bermuda job on page 127:

3333 Imperial Way
K-10004 Freetown
Fredonia

Mr Charles Fox
European Sales Office
ACME Atlantic Ltd
45 Pentonville Road
London EC2 4AC   13 May 1999

Dear Mr Fox,

I wish to apply for one of the positions described in your advertisement 'Work in Bermuda' in this week's Daily Planet.

I am 25 years old and a Fredonian citizen. I am at present working for Fredonian Enterprises, and as you know, we have been doing business with ACME Atlantic for a number of years.

My recent work has involved working in a team in the export department of my firm and I have developed confidence and skill in dealing with foreign buyers on the telephone and in writing, mainly using English.

My Fredonian is fluent, I speak and write reasonably good English and I can also handle business correspondence in German and Italian.

As you will see from my enclosed CV, my qualifications are good, and I think you will agree that my experience and language skills will help me to make a valuable contribution to your firm and you will find that I am an enthusiastic and resourceful employee.

I am available for interview at any time except for June 12th to 21st. My daytime phone number is 287 8889 extension 333.

I look forward to hearing from you,

Yours sincerely,

Jean Muster

Jean Muster

---

82 During the interview, make notes on each candidate's experience or potential under these headings:

CHECKLIST FOR INTERVIEWERS

Working under stress	*Working with other people*
Dealing with people in English	*Administration*
Travel	*Education and training*
Work experience	*Personality*
Health	*Present job*

83 You are the chief buyer for a mail order company or chain store. You know this salesperson well. Find out:

- the wholesale price of the product
- the recommended retail price of the product
- how quickly the goods could be shipped
- what kinds of customers the product would appeal to
- why your customers might find the product attractive
- how each item is packed
- if the product is supplied complete and ready to use
- where the product is manufactured

---

84 You are the OBSERVER.

As you listen to the conversation, make notes on these points:

- What kind of impression did each person make?
- If they sounded co-operative, how did this help the negotiation?
- If they sounded unhelpful, how did this affect the progress of the negotiation?
- What advice would you give the participants to improve their negotiating styles?
- How far was the transaction successful, in your opinion?
- Any other comments on their negotiation?

---

85 This is the letter you receive from Julio Martinez:

14 February 1999

Dear Sirs,

Account No. 645/A6D/03764/ Invoice No. 04276

I regret to inform you that the above invoice contains a mistake. It is almost certainly the case that the figure in the invoice for the total has been multiplied by a hundred. In view of our long-standing dealings with your company, I am convinced that you do not expect me to pay $81,648.00 for the last delivery of switches and electrical components.

As you know, anyway, from our recent phone call, we received only 25 gross switches. This means we still owe you money.

I would very much appreciate receiving a more reasonable invoice.

Sincerely yours,

Julio Martinez

Julio Martinez
Purchasing Dept.

Acknowledgements

The authors and publishers are grateful to the authors, publishers and others who have given permission for the use of copyright material identified in the text. In the cases where it has not been possible to identify the source of material used the publishers would welcome information from copyright owners.

p. 10 this article first appeared in *Business Life* magazine; p. 24 the computer screen by kind permission of Apple Computer Inc., copyright Apple Computer Inc., all rights reserved; p. 46 (*l*) Siemens AG, (*r*) Philipp Holzmann AG; p. 48 Business Books for the extract from *Maverick!* by Ricardo Semler; p. 51 cartoon from *Mrs Weber's Diary* by Posy Simmonds, published by Cape, reprinted by permission of the Peters Fraser & Dunlop Group Ltd; p. 66 article adapted from the *Financial Times* (18.9.92); p. 69 SITPRO © 1994; p. 70 reproduced by permission of Barclays Bank plc; p. 82 (*b*) Tim Felmingham of Axiom UK Ltd, (*r*) CE Software Incorporated (tel: 001 515 221 1801); p. 116 (*t*) Reader's Digest for the item from *How is it done?*, (*b*) Channel 4 Television for the item from *The Secret Life of the Office* by Tim Hunkin; p. 117 and p. 154 (File 26) *The Guardian* for the items from *eG Source Book*; pp. 121–2 Cadbury Limited for the text of the extract on tape and the diagram on p. 121 from *The Story of Cocoa and Chocolate* and for the extract on p. 122 from the brochure *The Story of Cadbury Limited*; p. 126 *The Guardian* for the article by Celia Weston (7.7.93) and p. 129 for the article by Jenny Ward (11.6.86); p. 155 (File 28) and p. 165 (File 58) Innovations (Mail Order) Limited.

For permission to include photographs, logos and other illustrative material:

pp. 8, 15, 28, 115, 120 (*tl, tc, tr*) Peter Lake; p. 9 Telegraph Colour Library; p. 11 Will Capel; p. 25 (*tl*) Zefa, (*tr*) Pictor, (*cl*) Rex Features, (*cr*) Pictor, (*bl*) Powerstock, (*br*) Pictor; p. 43 Bayer AG, Pepsi registered trade mark reproduced with the permission of PepsiCo Inc, BNP, British Airways, Sears, Roebuck and Co., Saab-Scania, Hilton International, Ford Motor Company Limited; p. 48 (*t*) Random House UK Ltd, (*c* and *b*) Semco SA; p. 52 (*l*) Peter Timmermans/Zefa, (*tr*) Zefa, (*br*) Clive Sawyer/Zefa; p. 55 Solar Electric Vehicle at Kew Gardens designed by Sir Norman Foster and Partners (photographer: Richard Davies); p. 62 Sunseeker International (Boats) Ltd; p. 65 Telegraph Colour Library (photographers: *tr* Ted Kurihara, *cl* Matt Lennert, *bl* M. J. Llorden); p. 66 Louis Vuitton; p. 88 (*tl*) Rio Othon Palace, Rio de Janeiro, Brazil, (*tr*) Caesar Park, Rio de Janeiro, Brazil; p. 94 Hotel Seiler au Lac, Interlaken; p. 96 Victoria State Opera, National Gallery of Victoria, The Victorian Business College; p. 99 (*tl* and *br*) Ogilvy & Mather Advertising Ltd (photographer: Andy Green), (*cl*) Ben & Jerry's ® Ice Cream, (*cr*) advertisement reproduced by permission of Michelin, (*bl*) Benetton SpA; p. 101 'global brands': Coca-Cola Great Britain and Ireland, Kellogg Company of Great Britain Limited (Kellogg's is a registered trade mark of Kellogg Company), McDonald's Restaurants Ltd, Kodak Limited, Rothmans (UK) Ltd, IBM Ltd, American Express Europe Ltd, Sony United Kingdom Limited, the three pointed star and the name 'Mercedes-Benz' are registered trade marks belonging to Mercedes-Benz AG

of Stuttgart, Germany, Nestlé UK Ltd (Nescafé is a registered trade mark of Société des Produits Nestlé SA); p.101 'luxury brands': Vendôme Luxury Group plc for the logo of Alfred Dunhill Limited, Louis Vuitton, Cartier Ltd, Vendôme Luxury Group plc for the logo of Montblanc Simplo Gmbh, La Chemise Lacoste; p. 101 (*br*) Leo Jones; p. 104 Swiss Tourist Office, Canadian Tourist Office, US Travel & Tourism Administration, Thai Tourist Authority, Austrian National Tourist Office, Irish Tourist Board, Japan National Tourist Organization; p. 112 (*tl* and *bl*) David Eckstein, (*tr*) Robin Summers, Summers Design Associates, (*br*) R B Bevan, University of Newcastle upon Tyne; pp. 120, 122 Cadbury Limited; p. 125 (*tl*) Rex Features, (*tr*) Popperfoto, (*bl*) Zefa, (*br*) Keith Hamshere/Rex Features/© LFL 1984 Lucasfilm Ltd; p. 126 Sunday Times/Rex Features; p. 127 Spectrum; p. 130 (*r*) Liverpool Students' Union, (*ct*) Thamesdown Borough Council, (*l*) Waltham Forest Borough Council, (*cb*) Liverpool City Council; p. 134 (*tl*) Judy Goldhill/Rex Features, (*tr*) Pictor, (*cr*) Powerstock, (*bl*) Craig McCormick/BTI, (*bc*) Bruce Ayres/Tony Stone Worldwide, (*br*) Pictor; p. 139 Pictor; p. 142 (*tr*) Sarah Almy, (*bl*) Telford Development Agency, (*br*) Wigan Metropolitan Borough Council Economic Development Office.

For permission to reproduce cartoons:

pp. 12, 17, 23, 34, 37, 40, 44, 49, 54, 64, 84, 103, 114, 117, 133, 145, 177 by kind permission of *Punch*; pp. 27, 141 © 1993 by Sidney Harris – *Harvard Business Review*; p. 76 Harley Schwadron – *Harvard Business Review*.

Illustrators:

pp. 7, 16, 26 (*t*), 28, 29, 39, 41 (*t*), 45, 49 (*t*), 52, 55, 71, 72, 78, 81, 87, 90, 100 (*b*), 102, 108, 110, 130, 137, 138, 139, 144 David Downton; pp. 13, 75 Max Ellis; pp. 26 (*b*), 27, 31 Philip Emms; pp. 33, 34 David Barnett; p. 41 (*b*) Michael Hill; p. 74 Peter Byatt; pp. 85, 86, 89 Annie Farrall; p. 92 Tony Coles; pp. 93, 104, 140, 143, 166, 169 Kathy Baxendale; p. 100 (*t*) Tracy Rich: pp. 106, 113 Diane Oliver.

(p. = page, *t* = top, *c* = centre, *b* = bottom, *r* = right, *l* = left)

Picture research by Amanda Ogden

Design and DTP by Newton Harris